CHILDHOOD OF W

JULIUS CAESAR

YOUNG STATESMAN

by Beatrice Gormley

Aladdin Paperbacks
New York   London   Toronto   Sydney

◐✦ ALADDIN PAPERBACKS
An imprint of Simon & Schuster Children's Publishing Division
1230 Avenue of the Americas, New York, NY 10020
Text copyright © 2006 by Beatrice Gormley
All rights reserved, including the right of reproduction in whole or in part in any form.
ALADDIN PAPERBACKS and colophon are trademarks of Simon & Schuster, Inc.
CHILDHOOD OF WORLD FIGURES is a registered trademark of Simon & Schuster, Inc.
Designed by Lisa Vega
The text of this book was set in Aldine 721.
Manufactured in the United States of America
First Aladdin Paperbacks edition June 2006
10 9 8 7 6 5 4 3 2 1
Library of Congress Control Number 2006923522
ISBN-13: 978-1-4169-1281-1
ISBN-10: 1-4169-1281-9

CONTENTS

Chapter 1 War Games 94–93 B.C.★★★★★★★★★★★★★★★★★★★1

Chapter 2 A World of Battles 92–91 B.C. ★★★★★★★★★★★17

Chapter 3 A War and a Wedding 90–89 B.C.★★★★★★★★33

Chapter 4 Attack on Rome 88 B.C. ★★★★★★★★★★★★★★50

Chapter 5 A Bride for Gaius 87 B.C.★★★★★★★★★★★★★★★65

Chapter 6 Gaius is a Man 87–85 B.C.★★★★★★★★★★★★★★81

Chapter 7 Everything Changes 85–84 B.C. ★★★★★★★★★98

Chapter 8 The Death List 83–82 B.C.★★★★★★★★★★★★★★120

Chapter 9 Run for Your Life 81 B.C.★★★★★★★★★★★★★★140

Chapter 10 The Citizen's Crown 80–77 B.C.★★★★★★★★★154

Chapter 11 Prisoner of Pirates 77–71 B.C.★★★★★★★★★★★168

Chapter 12 The Three-headed Monster 68–59 B.C.★★★190

Chapter 13   The Conquest of Gaul 58–52 B.C. ★★★★205

Chapter 14   Civil War 51–46 B.C. ★★★★★★★★★★★★★★★221

Chapter 15   The Dictator 46–44 B.C. ★★★★★★★★★★★236

              For More Information ★★★★★★★★★★★★★247

JULIUS
CAESAR

CHAPTER 1
WAR GAMES

94–93 B.C.

In the gardens of General Marius's mansion in Rome, a group of boys were playing war. The autumn day was warm and dry, and the boys wore tunics and sandals.

Young Marius, the general's son, was the oldest boy at fourteen. A red cloth hanging down his back marked him as the Roman commander. The boy beside him held a broomstick with a shingle fastened to the top, displaying an eagle and the letters SPQR. They stood for *Senatus Populusque Romanus,* the Senate and the People of Rome.

"Death to the Teutons!" shouted young Marius. He pointed dramatically with his wooden sword to the fountain in the middle of the garden. "Let the brook run red with Teuton blood!"

On the other side of the fountain, a boy stepped out from behind a column. Gaius was only six, the youngest in the group, but he held up his wooden sword to speak for the Teutons. "Truce, Marius! We don't want to play Teutons anymore."

"Do you surrender, then, Gaius?" demanded his cousin Marius. "I'll have a triumph parade, and you'll have to walk in chains behind my chariot. Then I'll have you executed."

"No," said the younger boy in a reasonable tone. "We don't want to be Teutons at all. We want to be Romans."

The boys in Marius's "army" burst out laughing, and the "Teutons" behind Gaius giggled too. A deep chortle was heard, and the boys looked up to see a man watching their game.

Under the arched entrance to the gardens, General Marius stood with legs apart and hands on his hips. He was wearing a plain tunic, but it was easy to see that he'd spent most of his life on military campaigns. His face, framed by receding gray hair, was grooved and rumpled like well-worn leather. The pale lines of scars crisscrossed his muscular arms and legs.

"If you're playing 'the Battle of Aquae Sextae,' of course you want to be Romans," said the general. "All the world—anyone who has any sense—would want to be Roman." He spit in the shrubbery as Gaius's mother had taught him *not* to do.

"But they can't be Romans, Father," exclaimed young Marius. "If everyone was a Roman, there wouldn't be anyone to fight. How could we capture any slaves or seize any booty?"

"No one to fight?" Sextus Caesar, another of Gaius's uncles, had come up behind General Marius. "Nonsense. We Romans can always fight among ourselves, eh, Marius?" Laughing heartily, he slapped the general on the back.

"Master, excuse me." A blond, blue-eyed man, a slave, approached General Marius and bowed. "Dinner is ready."

"The war's over, boys," said the general, jerking his head in the direction of the dining hall. "Son," he added to young Marius, pointing a finger for emphasis, "you want to win the war? Keep your troops well fed. After the war, give them land. Treat your soldiers right, and they'll treat you right. That's the secret."

"Yes, Father," said young Marius carelessly. But Gaius was listening.

At dusk, the family party was over. Gaius's family—his father, Gaius Julius Caesar; his mother, Aurelia; and his sister, Julia Minor— left Uncle Marius's mansion on the Palatine Hill. Uncle Marius sent slaves with torches to guide their litters down the steep, winding street. He also sent half a dozen hulking body-guards to escort them home because it was dangerous to be out in the city at night. Julia Minor rode in one litter with their father while

Gaius climbed into the other litter with his mother.

"Mother, Uncle Marius's house is much bigger and nicer than ours, isn't it?" asked Gaius.

"It's bigger," admitted his mother. "Even the *lararium* is bigger." The *lararium* was the family shrine. "In our house, it's a cabinet, but in theirs, it's a separate room, like a temple."

"I wish we lived in that house," said Gaius.

Aurelia didn't answer for a moment, and Gaius tried to read her expression in the dark. Then she asked, "Did you look inside the *lararium*?"

"Yes," said Gaius. He'd stepped between marble pillars to peer into the shrine. "There's a painting on the wall, of a priest leading a bull."

"Yes, a fine painting. Uncle Marius must have paid a great deal of money for it. But did you see any ancestors?"

Gaius thought a moment. The *lararium* cabinet at home held the masks of their ancestors, including Grandfather Cotta's, who had been consul of Rome. Consul was the highest office in the Roman government. "No, I didn't," Gaius answered his mother.

"No, of course not," said Aurelia, "because General Marius's parents were poor laborers, while we are patricians." Her voice was calm and cultured, as usual. "Did you notice the mosaic of the Birth of Venus in Marius's atrium? A showy work of art, but you have something much better. You are *descended* from the goddess Venus. She was the mother of your ancestor Aeneas."

The litter rocked and tilted along the streets as Gaius took this in. Then an idea struck him, and he asked, "When Uncle Marius dies, will *he* be a famous ancestor?"

"He already is," said Aurelia with a smile in her voice. "That's why your cousin Marius struts and preens, because his father is a hero. But will young Marius himself grow up to be a hero? We shall see." She took Gaius's face in her hands. "As for you, my dear son, you can surely become someone's hero, if you strive for that prize. Remember that Venus is your protector. She'll bring you good fortune and guide you to your destiny."

The next summer, Gaius was almost seven, old enough to learn to read and write. Every morning now he got up before dawn to get ready for school.

Myro, the slave who looked after Gaius, helped him dress in a loincloth, tunic, and shoes. Gaius was already wearing his *bulla*, a gold amulet on a cord. All children had to wear a *bulla*, even if it was only a leather pouch with charms inside to protect them from demons and bad luck.

This morning was the Kalends—the first day of the month—of June of the 661st year since the founding of Rome. Every morning the family gathered for prayers, but since this was the Kalends, Father also sacrificed a pig to the household gods.

Then, with Myro carrying Gaius's school

satchel, the boy and the slave left the house. "A good day at school to you, Master Gaius," said the doorkeeper. He unbarred the front door to let them out.

Early sunshine brightened the upper stories of the buildings along the Subura Way. Most of the Subura, the section of Rome where the Caesars lived, was made up of apartment buildings rather than separate houses like the Caesars'. The ground floors of these tenements were used for shops, such as the butcher shop they were passing now. The summer day was hot already, and the pen beside the butcher's gave off a rank barnyard stink.

Gaius ducked under the props holding up one tenement building. There were long cracks in the unpainted wall, and the mortar patching the cracks was falling out. Gaius peered at the letters scrawled alongside the biggest crack.

Gaius could read some words, and he could even write a few. For instance, he could write his name, Gaius Julius Caesar. Gaius was his private name, just for family and good friends. "Julius" meant that his family belonged to the Julian clan. And Caesar, his surname, meant that Gaius belonged to the Caesar family: Father, Mother, his sisters Julia Major and Julia Minor, Uncle Sextus Caesar and his household, and Father's cousin Lucius Caesar and his household.

Of the words on the tenement wall, though, Gaius could read only "wall," "our," and "him." "What does that say, Myro?"

Myro shrugged. "You know I can't read, Master Gaius. Do I look like a Greek teacher?"

"I'll tell you what it says," called a voice over their heads. They looked up to see a man's face with three days' stubble at a second-floor window. "It says, 'May this wall collapse on our villain landlord and cause him a lingering death!'"

A woman stuck her head out the next window of the tenement. "You fool, how could the wall fall on the landlord? He never comes here—he just sends his man around to collect the rent. Anyway, shut up. My kids are sleeping."

Gaius wanted to stay and hear what the man

would say back, but Myro pulled him along. "You'll be late for lessons. Do you want the teacher to switch you with his birch rod? I don't want your lady mother scolding *me*."

They came to a bakery, fragrant with fresh bread, and Myro and Gaius stopped to buy a roll for breakfast. They passed a tavern, shuttered and barred at this hour, with its sour-wine smell. Farther down the street was Gratus the carriage-maker's shop, smelling like wood shavings and iron. The carriage-maker was just opening the doors of his yellow-painted shop.

"Good morning, Citizen Gratus," said Gaius. He knew the carriage-maker, a friendly man. But even if he hadn't, he would have known Gratus was a Roman citizen by the iron ring on his hand. "I'm going to school, and then I'm going to the Forum with Father. He's running for praetor."

"Good morning, young Gaius Caesar," said Gratus. "I'm glad you reminded me about the election—there's something I meant to do.

Mind your teacher and watch out for that switch, now!"

Back home after school, Gaius ate a quick lunch of bread and cheese and let Myro dress him for the Forum. He stepped out the front door behind his father, and his father's retinue of clients fell into place around them. Now that Senator Caesar was running for the office of praetor, or judge, he needed an impressive following of clients, or people who owed him favors. The clients were expected to wait outside their patron's house and accompany him in public.

Gaius's father was wearing his senator's tunic, with two broad purple stripes down the front, the red shoes that only patricians (the higher nobility) were allowed to wear, and his man's toga. Men's togas were normally the off-white color of unbleached wool. But since Senator Caesar was running for a public office, his toga was chalk white.

Gaius walked behind his father, wearing a clean white tunic and his boy's toga, with its purple border. Gaius was proud that he handled the heavy, awkward toga so well. There were no pins or clasps to fasten a toga—the final fold over the left shoulder had to be held in place with the left hand. His father's valet had folded and draped the woolen cloth just so over Gaius's tunic, and now Gaius was supposed to keep it that way for the rest of the day.

Down the Subura Way, Gratus the carriage-maker was putting the finishing touches on a sign. Black letters on the yellow wall of his shop urged: G. JULIUS CEASAR FOR PRAETOR. He smiled and bowed as Gaius and his father went by. "Good luck to you, Senator Caesar," he called. "And to your fine young son."

Gaius's father lifted a hand in greeting to the carriage-maker, and he nodded to the freedman carrying his money pouch. The man paused to put a few coins in Gratus's hand.

Senator Caesar and his retinue continued down the Subura Way to the foot of Palatine

Hill and past the round Temple of Vesta. Uncle Cotta was waiting for them in the portico of the Regia, the office building for the College of Pontiffs.

Gaius's father and Uncle Cotta, brothers-in-law, gave each other a formal hug, and Uncle Cotta fell into step with the group. "I think you can count on the bakers' guild and the fullers'," he said to Gaius's father, "as long as they can expect a pig roast after your victory."

"Excellent!" said Gaius's father. "I sent my freedman Marcellus down to Arpinum yesterday to make sure Marius's country neighbors come to Rome for the election. Can we provide tents for them on the Field of Mars?"

Gaius Caesar the Elder and his retinue made their way through the crowds in the Forum, the great paved square at the center of Rome. Besides the usual throng of shoppers, vendors, officials, businessmen, beggars, and idlers, the Forum was dotted with candidates in chalk-white togas. Each candidate trailed a retinue of relatives, clients, and hangers-on.

Gaius's father greeted each shopkeeper and his customers in the arcade along the Basilica Aemelia, but he kept moving. Gaius would have liked to stop and look at the Shrine of Janus, the double-faced god, and the Rostra, the speaker's platform that was decorated with the rams of captured enemy warships. But he had a serious part to play today, and he kept close behind his father.

At the Senate building, a number of men in senators' togas were gathered on the steps. Gaius's father stopped to greet them all, including his brother, Sextus Caesar, and his cousin Lucius Caesar. The summer sun shone hot on the stone pavement, and Gaius's woolen toga made his neck itch. But he didn't scratch or squirm. The important thing was not for Gaius to be comfortable. The important thing was to have all the voters in Rome admire Gaius Julius Caesar and his fine young son.

"So this is Gaius Caesar the Younger," said one of the senators, stooping in front of the boy. "What do you have to say for yourself, eh?"

Gaius answered in a polite but firm voice, "I say, 'Vote for Gaius Julius Caesar for praetor,' sir!"

Another man in the group ruffled Gaius's hair. "You want us to vote for your father for praetor? Tell me, what exactly does a praetor do?"

The other men turned to listen. They were smiling—they thought Gaius wouldn't be able to answer.

Standing very straight, his left hand holding his toga in place, Gaius said, "A praetor passes judgment in a court of law, sir." He glanced around the group, meeting each man's gaze for an instant. "My father is wise and fair, so he'll be a very good judge." He finished with a forthright smile.

The senators raised their eyebrows, and one of them clapped Gaius on the shoulder. "Well said!" He added to Gaius's father, "Quite a little politician you have there."

"But why should your father want to hold public office, lad?" the first man asked. "Why not move out to the country, settle down in a peaceful villa, and enjoy life instead of bothering with politics?"

Gaius knew the man was teasing him, but again he answered seriously. "Because Roman senators have a higher duty, to run the government. Other nations let kings rule, but Rome is special. Rome is a republic, governed by the Senate and the People's Assembly."

"There you go." Uncle Cotta folded his arms, nodding and beaming. "The boy said it all."

CHAPTER 2
A WORLD OF BATTLES

92–91 B.C.

With the support of the bakers' and the fullers' guilds, the farmers in Arpinum, all the connections of the Julian clan, and the influence of Old Marius, Gaius Caesar the Elder won his election. Next January, he took office as praetor. On court days he processed into the Forum with six lictors, special attendants for officials, marching ahead of him. Praetor Caesar took his seat on a stone dais underneath a canopy.

Once in a while, as a special treat, Gaius's uncle Cotta took him to the Forum to watch a trial. Uncle Cotta's slaves set up folding chairs for them near the dais, and a large audience gathered behind them. All Romans enjoyed a trial, especially if there weren't any plays or games going on. Gaius's uncle quizzed him on the Twelve Tables, the ancient Roman laws, while they were waiting for the court to open. But Gaius didn't mind, because he could rattle off the Twelve Tables with no trouble.

That March, Gaius's cousin Marius became a man. He put away his *bulla*, dressed for the first time in a man's borderless toga, and registered to vote. Soon after that, young Marius married a girl named Licinia.

Gaius was too young to attend the wedding banquet, but he heard his parents talking about what a good match Uncle Marius had arranged. Licinia was the daughter of Lucius Licinius Crassus, a leader of the conservative politicians. General Marius was a reformer, demanding land for his veterans and voting rights for Italians outside Rome. A marriage between the two families was a good sign for Roman politics, as well as for Marius and his family.

This year, the family worked on getting

Uncle Sextus, Father's brother, elected to consul. This office was so important that people dated events by consulships; they said, "In the year that Lucius Aurelius Cotta was consul . . ." Signs urging S. JULIUS CAESAR FOR CONSUL appeared on walls all over Rome, including Gratus the carriage-maker's shop. Uncle Sextus arranged for a day of gladiatorial games to be staged in the Forum, free of charge to voting citizens. He paid the town criers to shout his name from the seven hills of the city.

For his campaign, Uncle Sextus rented a *nomenclator*, a specially trained slave to remember people's names and connections for him. When Uncle Sextus went out in public, the slave stayed close by, whispering advice in his ear: "Here comes Spiros, a wealthy merchant from Sicily. Although he can't vote, he'll contribute money if he thinks you'll support full citizenship rights for Sicilians."

Gaius was embarrassed for his uncle that he needed a *nomenclator*. Uncle Sextus wasn't blind and deaf, after all! Why couldn't he remember the face, the name, and the connections of everyone he'd ever met? Gaius's mother, Aurelia, could. Gaius was getting good at it, himself.

Again, the Caesar family won their election. On the Kalends of January, a cold, bright day, Sextus Julius Caesar was installed as consul. Gaius, his father, Uncle Marius, other family members, friends, clients, as well as the priests and a bull for the sacrifice joined Uncle Sextus's procession through the Forum. The Vestal Virgins, the priestesses who tended the sacred fire in the Temple of Vesta, also honored the ceremony with their presence.

Everyone in Gaius's family was glowing with pride; Uncle Sextus was the Caesar family's first consul in sixty-five years. The procession left the Forum and began to climb the steep ramp up Capitoline Hill. The Temple of Jupiter crowned the hill, and there, Consul Sextus would start the year properly by sacrificing to the patron god of Rome.

The procession passed the Temple of Honor

and Courage, commemorating Marius's victories. A crowd of commoners on the temple steps cheered General Marius even more than they did the new consul. "Old Man! Old Man!" That had been his army's nickname for General Marius. The general smiled and waved from his open litter.

As Gaius mounted the ramp, he gazed over a widening panorama. The mansions of Palatine Hill overlooked the red-tiled roofs of the Forum. On the other side of Capitoline Hill shimmered the blue snake of the Tiber River, banded by bridges. Shading his eyes, Gaius looked south to the racetrack of the Circus Maximus. Beyond the city wall, the Appian Way stretched into the distance.

Suddenly a bellow rang out. Was it the sacrificial bull? No—Uncle Marius. The whole procession halted in front of an imposing new gilded sculpture. Sunlight glaring on the gold made Gaius blink.

What was the matter? New statues, trophies, and posters were always appearing in public places around the city. But Gaius had never seen Uncle Marius scowl at any of them like that. The old warrior's face was beet-red.

Squinting at the sculpture, Gaius saw a man in military breastplate, kilt, and cloak, with a crested helmet under his arm. A laurel wreath, a token of victory, crowned his head. One booted foot rested on the neck of a kneeling captive.

Wiggling to the front of the group, Gaius read the inscription on the base of the sculpture:

L. CORNELIUS SULLA
VICTOR OVER JUGURTHA

No wonder Uncle Marius was sputtering so that spit came out of his mouth instead of words. Gaius had heard many times the story of how Uncle Marius won the war in Numidia. *Marius*, not Sulla, was the one to whom the Senate had allowed a triumph, a victory parade through Rome. The enemy king Jugurtha of Numidia, in chains, had followed Old Marius's chariot.

"The nerve of Sulla!" exclaimed Aunt Julia. "As if *he'd* won the Jurgurthian War!"

Gaius looked at his father. Gaius Caesar the Elder shook his head, but he looked more worried than angry. "This means trouble," he muttered.

As Uncle Sextus's term as consul began, G. Julius Caesar's term as praetor had come to an end. Now his duties as governor of Asia Minor began—as soon as he could get to his province. The journey would take weeks. Governor Caesar couldn't even start off until March, when the winter storms were over and ships could sail the Mediterranean again.

The day before Gaius Caesar the Elder left Rome, Gaius stepped into his father's office. His father was going over last-minute instructions with his steward. A large map was spread out on the table, the curled edges weighted with bronze seals and ink bottles. "Come and listen, Gaius," said Caesar the Elder. "I expect you to write me regular reports too."

Gaius's father went on to the steward, "I've marked this map so you'll know where to send your reports during the next month or so." He ran his finger down Italy from Rome to Capua. Gaius knew about Capua, where the best gladiators trained. He craned his neck to look over the steward's shoulder at the parchment map.

"Best not to send anything to me at Capua," Gaius's father went on. "If something comes up in the next few days, post your letter straight on to Brundisium." He slid his finger across boot-shaped Italy to a city on the heel. "I'll be there at least two or three days, loading the ships and waiting for a favorable wind."

If the winds were fair, a day's sailing would take Gaius's father and his ships from Brundisium across the Adriatic Sea. Then he'd sail around the coast of Greece to Athens, on the

Aegean Sea. In the *Iliad*, the story of the Trojan War, the Greek king Agamemnon had launched his fleet into the Aegean toward Troy.

"After Athens," Gaius's father was telling the steward, "the next mailing should go to—"

"Troy," breathed Gaius. "I wish I could come!"

His father frowned at the interruption. "I'm not going to Asia Minor for pleasure, son. I'm going to govern a province for Rome."

"I know, sir," said Gaius quickly. "And for our family, too." He wasn't nine years old yet, but he knew that governors could make a lot of money. The Caesars needed money for many things: a dowry for Julia Minor, a pony for Gaius, a full-time scribe . . .

His father smiled a bit wistfully. "Well, who knows—I might get a chance to visit the ruins of Troy. If I do, I'll send you a souvenir." Turning back to the steward, Gaius Caesar the Elder traced a route across the Aegean from Athens, Greece, to Ephesus on the coast of Asia

Minor. "From then on, unless I tell you otherwise, send all letters to my headquarters in Ephesus."

As Gaius's father discussed other matters with the steward, Gaius bent over the parchment on the table. From the northern shore of the Mediterranean Sea, the peninsula of Italy hung down like a man's leg. In the far west, the knob of Spain touched the border of the map. Uncle Marius had been governor of Spain before he married Aunt Julia. Beyond Spain was the ocean, and . . . no one knew what else.

Africa was dotted with battle sites, including Numidia and Mauritania, where Uncle Marius (not Sulla!) had won the Jugurthian War. Far in the East there was the battlefield of Issus, where Alexander the Great had defeated the Persians three hundred years ago. A painting in Uncle Marius's office showed Alexander riding into battle.

The next day, Gaius, Aurelia, and Julia Minor, as well as a crowd of other family, friends, and clients, accompanied his father to the Capena Gate and the beginning of the Appian Way. A troop of mounted soldiers waited for the governor outside the walls, because armed soldiers were not allowed in the city of Rome. Neither were military uniforms, so Gaius's father had waited until now to don his commander's cape. Under the gray March skies, the cape glowed bright red.

Gaius's life went on much the same as when his father was home. He spent the mornings at school. Afternoons, if the weather was good, he often walked across the city and out the Fontinal Gate to the Field of Mars.

There was always something happening on the Field of Mars. For one thing, the Field was the place where soldiers drilled, outside the city walls. Chariot racers also practiced here, and youths trained with swords and spears. Gaius usually brought a leather ball along and looked for other boys to play trigon.

Gaius liked trigon, a kind of three-cornered game of catch with two balls. The faster and trickier the other players, the more fun. Usually Gaius was the last player left when the game broke up. He once tried to get the other boys to add a third ball and a fourth player, to make trigon even more interesting. But they didn't want to change the rules.

One afternoon a few months after his father had left, Gaius and his mother sat in the courtyard. The air was hot and still, even in the shade, but Aurelia's maid fanned them with a reed fan. Gaius's mother spun wool into thread while Gaius wrote a letter to his father. Aurelia didn't have to spin or weave—they could buy cloth in the Forum markets—but spinning was supposed to be a proper thing for a Roman matron to do.

Gaius read his mother the words scratched into the wax at the top of his tablet: "'From Gaius Julius Caesar the Younger to his father, Gaius Julius Caesar, the governor of Asia Minor, at Ephesus, greetings. I hope you are well. Mother, Julia Major, Julia Minor, and I are well.'"

Aurelia nodded. "Very nice." She let the spindle weight fall, twisting and smoothing the thread between her fingers.

"'I went to the Field of Mars yesterday for riding lessons,'" Gaius read on. "'The cavalry officer praised my riding.'"

"Porcius," the officer had told another boy, "look at the way Gaius Caesar rides, without kicking or whipping his horse. For Neptune's sake, the horse isn't your enemy!"

Gaius rested his stylus as he remembered something else: the new face in the Forum. Gaius had gone there with Cousin Lucius to listen to a tribune named Drusus. Then heads had turned from the speaker to stare at this man.

"See that arrogant fellow with the wreath on his head?" Cousin Lucius whispered in Gaius's ear. "That's Sulla. So he's back from Cilicia, where he was governor."

Now, sitting in the courtyard with his letter half finished, Gaius decided not to write about Sulla. What had struck him the most about

Sulla was the impression he made on everyone around him. Whereas Gaius's father seemed to blend into a group and disappear, Sulla made all eyes look at him. Sulla Felix, Sulla the Lucky, his soldiers called him. They thought Sulla's good luck rubbed off on them.

Skipping over Sulla, Gaius described the speech that Tribune Drusus had made on voting rights for the Italians. The reform faction had gotten into a shouting match with the conservatives. Conservative senators thought Drusus had gone too far, Cousin Lucius said, trying to give the Italian allies full citizenship. They also thought Drusus wanted power only for himself.

The Italian allies, on the other hand, thought the senators wanted power only for themselves. There had been big demonstrations lately, with throngs of Italians marching through the streets and into the Forum. "We want the vote!" they shouted. "We want it now!"

This was a lot to write. Gaius wiggled his

fingers, cramped from gripping the stylus. "When I'm a man," he remarked to his mother, "I'll dictate all my letters to my scribe."

Aurelia smiled at him. "All right, that's enough writing. I'll tell your father the family news in my letter."

Gaius wrote his closing: *The Kalends of June, in the year of Sextus Caesar's consulship, from Rome.* He handed the two-sided tablet to his mother. "How long will it be before Father reads this?"

"Well, let me think." Aurelia set down her spindle, took the stylus, and began writing her own message with quick, neat scratches. She could write and talk at the same time. "We'll give our letter to Cousin Lucius, and he'll give it to the Senate's courier to put in the mail pouch for Asia Minor. They leave every few days, usually. . . ."

Aurelia's voice trailed off, and they both turned their heads toward the front of the house. "Brother," she exclaimed, "what is it?" The tablet slid from her lap as she jumped up.

Uncle Cotta stood on the low porch, leaning on a column. "Tribune Drusus has been assassinated."

Assassinated. Tribunes had been assassinated before, Gaius knew. But those events were history, not the kind of thing Gaius expected to happen now.

"How dare they?" whispered Aurelia. "The person of the tribune is sacred."

"I'm not surprised that they dared to do it," Uncle Cotta said heavily, "but I don't understand how it happened. Apparently Drusus was standing outside his house on Palatine Hill, talking with his friends and clients. Suddenly, he slumped down—stabbed in the ribs."

"They must have bought one of Drusus's so-called friends," said Aurelia grimly. "The worst thing is, the Italians will never stand for this. Drusus was their last hope. Now they'll go to war for their rights."

CHAPTER 3

A WAR AND A WEDDING

90–89 B.C.

Aurelia was right: The Italian cities tried to break away from Rome. The war went on through the autumn and into the new year. The Forum seemed empty and quiet, with many of the men Gaius knew having left to fight the rebels. Cousin Lucius Caesar was elected consul, and during his term a compromise was reached. Rome granted citizenship to the Italian cities, except for any who were still in rebellion against Rome.

Speaking in the Forum, Cousin Lucius praised the Romans for their wise and generous action. In private, Gaius heard him exclaim, "Why couldn't we have given them citizenship to begin with? It would have saved a lot of trouble."

Amid the turmoil of Lucius Caesar's consulship, Gaius's father returned from Asia Minor. He did come back with coffers full of gold, as they'd hoped. Now the family could afford a scribe, a decent dowry for Julia Minor, and a Spanish pony for Gaius. Aurelia hired a well-known artist to paint the family's portrait, and she had the painting hung in the dining room.

Gaius's father even thought about moving to a house in a better neighborhood, but Aurelia talked him out of it. "Better to spend the money on Gaius's education. He should have a really good tutor, and later he ought to study in Greece."

"Isn't he young to study with a tutor?" asked Gaius Caesar the Elder.

"I suppose so, but Gaius already knows everything an ordinary teacher could teach him," answered Aurelia. "He knows the Twelve Tables of Roman law backward and forward.

You've heard him recite Xenophon's debate between Pleasure and Virtue. He's read every book in our house, including Cato the Censor's dull text on farming."

Gaius's father asked Aurelia's brother, Gaius's uncle Cotta, to take over the next stage of his education. Gaius thought Uncle Cotta was a little pompous, but he was certainly a highly educated man. He seemed to know all about wars and art, politics and drama, and how they connected with one another. On a walk around Rome with Gaius one day, he stopped at a shrine to Alexander the Great. "Always honor Alexander, Gaius," he said. "Do you know why I say that?"

Gaius looked up at his uncle in surprise. "Because Alexander the Great conquered the world."

Uncle Cotta held up a forefinger. "Ah, everyone thinks that. But Alexander's true achievement was to spread the blessings of Greek civilization throughout the world. Study your Greek, my boy. The Greeks had the finest sculptors and architects, the best poets and playwrights, the wisest philosophers."

Gaius smiled to himself. That wasn't the way Uncle Marius talked about the Greeks. "Greeks!" Gaius had heard the old general snort, the time Aunt Julia tried to get him to take her to the performance of a Greek drama. "What do those slaves have to teach us?" Since the Romans had conquered the Greeks, Marius figured, the Greeks couldn't be that important.

Uncle Cotta's politics were a little different from Marius's, too. He was friendly with many of the conservative senators, including Sulla. "I know how Old Marius feels about Sulla, but the man's an outstanding general," said Uncle Cotta. "And he has outstanding taste in art."

No one ever said Marius had outstanding taste, thought Gaius. Marius's favorite kind of entertainment was a comedy in which the actors beat one another over the head with enormous sausages. He also liked acrobats, while Uncle Cotta called them "fellows jumping around like trained dogs."

But Gaius admired acrobats. If you stood up close to watch them, you could see how strong they were, their muscles bunching to catapult them into the air. You could also see how easily an acrobat could break his neck if his timing was off.

Uncle Cotta could be stuffy, but Gaius liked going around the city with him. Rome was crammed with fine statues and paintings and captured trophies brought back from distant lands, and Uncle Cotta knew the story of each one. He knew the history and legends behind every feature of Rome itself, for that matter.

For instance, there was the Lacus Curtius, a twelve-sided, stone-rimmed pool in the middle of the Forum, near the speakers' platform. It was no bigger than the pool in the Caesars' atrium. But Uncle Cotta said that hundreds of years ago, the Lacus Curtius used to be a lake covering most of the Forum. The lake was named, the legend went, after Marcus Curtius, the greatest warrior in Rome. He had sacrificed himself for the power and glory of Rome.

Gaius looked at the small pool. "If Marcus Curtius sacrificed himself for Rome, shouldn't he have a bigger monument?"

"Perhaps," said his uncle. "On the other hand, you might say that *Rome* is his monument."

The next year, Pompeius Strabo took office as consul. He was also commander of the Roman army in the war against the rebels, which dragged on in some areas. Pompeius Strabo put his son Gnaeus Pompeius on his staff, as well as a youth named Marcus Cicero. Sulla, the general Uncle Marius hated, also led Romans into battle against the Italians.

That same year, Gaius's sister Julia Minor married Marcus Atius Balbus. Julia Minor was thirteen, the same age at which their older sister, Julia Major, had been married several years before. Julia Minor's marriage had been decided on after careful discussion by the Caesar family council, and in a formal meeting of the Caesars with the Balbus family. Marcus

Balbus's family wasn't patrician, like the Caesars, but he was wealthy. And he was well connected: Consul Pompeius Strabo was his uncle.

The day before the wedding, Aurelia and the household slaves rushed around, busy with preparations. Gaius found Julia Minor sitting on a bench in the Caesars' little garden, looking forlorn. "I don't mind getting married," she told her brother, "but I wish I didn't have to leave our house." She twisted her engagement ring, gold with clasped hands, on the fourth finger of her left hand. "We hardly ever see Julia Major anymore."

Gaius felt sorry for her. Children always had to do what their families decided for them, but girls seemed to have even less choice than boys. He tried to think of something comforting. "Look at Aunt Julia—she sees her brothers and cousins all the time."

"Well, of course people come to see her! She's married to the great general Marius, elected consul six times! They want her to put in a good word for them with her husband."

Gaius knew that was true. "Look at Mother, then. Uncle Cotta and Cousin Cotta think the world of her."

"Mother's different," said Julia Minor. "She can do anything."

Gaius didn't have a good answer to that. He was beginning to realize that their mother, Aurelia, was indeed a special woman. She knew exactly what was going on in the Forum—the politics, the business, the comings and goings of important Romans and foreigners. When she gave her opinion in her quiet, cultured voice, the men in the family listened to her.

Gaius tried to think of something to cheer his sister up. "Wait till I'm a man. I'll be elected praetor, like Father, and then I'll be appointed governor of a province. I'll make your son my first assistant."

"Oh, that's very comforting," said Julia Minor. "I only have to wait until *you* grow up, and then until my son grows up!"

They laughed together, but Gaius saw tears

shining in his sister's eyes. He longed to say something to make her feel better. He held up his hand to make a solemn vow. "I swear by our ancestors: If I don't have a son of my own, your son will be my heir."

Julia Minor shivered. "Don't speak of not having a son! You'll bring yourself bad luck." Then she smiled and touched his cheek. "You're a good brother, Gaius."

That afternoon the augurs, religious officials who read omens, arrived to make sure the signs predicted a favorable day for Julia Minor's wedding. The auguries were good, and so the next day the relatives of the bride and groom crammed themselves into the Caesars' small atrium. Gaius teetered on the rim of the pool to watch Julia Minor, her hair done in a bride's special braids and ribbons under her flame-colored veil, join hands with Marcus Balbus.

Normally there would have been a wedding feast at the bride's parents' house. But some of the most important guests, including Uncle

Marius and Consul Pompeius Strabo, the groom's uncle, were in the army and couldn't enter Rome. So Balbus gave the feast at his villa on the banks of the Tiber, just outside the city.

Since it was a special occasion, the older children of both families helped serve at the feast. "This is a good chance for you to talk with some important people," Aurelia advised her son beforehand.

Moving through the dining hall with a pitcher, Gaius first poured wine for a former consul's son, Marcus Licinius Crassus. Crassus, a man in his midtwenties, was also an officer in the army. "Congratulations to you and your family," Crassus said, lifting his cup to Gaius. He winked. "They must be looking for a bride for you now, eh?"

Gaius shrugged and grinned. He knew that Publius Crassus, Marcus's father, had been consul several years ago. Now he was censor, another important government position. Crassus's family weren't patricians, but they were distantly related to a notable Roman, the late Crassus the Orator. Another thing to remember about Crassus's family was that they supported Sulla, not Marius. But that was no reason not to be friendly.

At the table next to Marcus Crassus was the head couch, occupied by Consul Pompeius Strabo, uncle of the groom. Next to the consul was his son, Gnaeus Pompeius, or Pompey. People said he was a young man to watch. He was only seventeen, but already one of his father's advisers.

It would be convenient, thought Gaius, if his own father was elected consul and could give *him* a boost up the political ladder. But would Gaius Caesar the Elder ever rise to the position of consul? Gaius was beginning to doubt it.

Pompey kept touching the lock of hair that fell over his forehead, as if he thought he was a fine-looking fellow. Holding up his cup for Gaius to refill, he gave him a kindly smile. "So, now our families are connected! You seem like an able lad. Come see me in a few years, after your manhood ceremony."

Gaius thanked him, bowing slightly before moving on with the wine pitcher. Pompey was a bit full of himself, wasn't he? thought Gaius. His father might be consul, but he was only a member of the lower nobility.

One mild September morning while the war with the Italian allies was still dragging on, a letter arrived at the Caesars' house from the distinguished Quintus Mucius Scaevola, Chief Pontiff. Scaevola invited them to his home to hear Gnipho, a famous rhetorician from Alexandria, demonstrate the art of persuasion. Also, some promising young orators would take turns giving practice speeches and dramatic recitations.

Gaius's father was going to his vineyards to check up on the grape harvest, and ordinarily he would have taken Gaius with him to the country. But Aurelia persuaded him to let the boy go to Scaevola's reception with her instead. "Gaius will learn so much."

Uncle Cotta, a friend of the Chief Pontiff, escorted them to Scaevola's mansion on Palatine Hill. Scaevola's house was as luxurious as Uncle Marius's—"but in better taste," remarked Aurelia, exchanging a smile with her brother. "Look at that African marble." She gestured at the columns in the portico. "What it must have cost to ship it across the sea!"

In the garden, Scaevola himself greeted Aurelia, Gaius, and Cotta. He introduced them to Gnipho the Rhetorician, a dignified man with short-trimmed hair and beard. When the guests were all seated comfortably, Scaevola spoke to the gathering.

"Honored friends, as you know, today we have the privilege of listening to the distinguished rhetorician Marcus Antonius Gnipho. But first, I want you to hear a talented young man with a deep feeling for our traditional Roman values. Recently he served gallantly on

General Pompeius Strabo's staff in the struggle against the Italian rebels." He gestured toward a thin youth standing beside a column. "Marcus Tullius Cicero will deliver Cato the Censor's famous speech."

Gaius remembered Marcus Cicero; he was one of the youths who used to train on the Field of Mars with Cousin Marius. Unlike young Marius, Cicero hadn't seemed to enjoy weapons practice very much. Now, grown taller and scrawnier, he looked even less like a soldier. While Crassus was introducing him, he swallowed nervously, making the Adam's apple bob in his long, thin neck. But once Cicero began to speak, he seemed confident.

Gaius had heard that speech of Cato's before; in fact, Gaius's teacher had made the class memorize part of it. But he'd never gotten all the feeling and meaning that came across now from Cicero. This skinny youth seemed to turn into a statesman standing before the Senate sixty years ago, reminding the Romans of the horrors of the wars with Carthage.

All Roman schoolchildren knew about those wars. Carthage had been a powerful kingdom on the north coast of Africa. The Carthaginian general, Hannibal, led his army all the way through Spain into Gaul. He crossed the Alps—with elephants!—and invaded Italy as far south as Cannae.

Uncle Marius always spoke admiringly of Hannibal, even though he'd been an enemy. "Speed and surprise, boys," he'd told Gaius and his cousins more than once. "Hannibal knew how to use speed and surprise, and by Hercules, he almost conquered us."

Hannibal was halted only by an even greater Roman general, Scipio Africanus. But it was Cato the Censor, who, years after Hannibal, caused Carthage's final defeat. Visiting Carthage on an official mission, Cato became convinced that Carthage was getting ready to attack Rome once more. He returned to Rome with this conclusion: "Carthage must be destroyed."

Gaius had never thought Cato the Censor's

speeches were exciting, but now the old Roman's words came alive in Cicero's mouth. Gaius could see Hannibal's ferocious warriors and their monstrous elephants pouring over the northern mountains. The hair stood up on the back of Gaius's neck as he listened to Cicero declaim one more time, "Carthage must be destroyed."

Finished with his recitation, Cicero stood with his head bowed. The courtyard was silent for a moment, and then the audience broke into applause. Aurelia commented to Uncle Cotta, "What a remarkable youth! And his family comes from the country, don't they?"

After the recital was over, slaves moved through the company serving cold drinks and tidbits. The courtyard buzzed with conversation. A small crowd gathered around Marcus Cicero, complimenting him on his speech. Gnipho told him, "I hope you'll think about going to Rhodes to study. I'd be glad to write you a recommendation to Apollonius—he's the best rhetorician there is, in my opinion." Cicero beamed.

Waiting his turn, Gaius stepped up to congratulate Marcus Cicero. "When I'm a general," he told him with a smile, "I hope you'll talk the Senate into backing *my* war!"

The older boy laughed and raised his eyebrows, as if trying to imagine Gaius commanding legions of soldiers. "*When* you're a general," he answered, "it'll be a pleasure."

CHAPTER 4
ATTACK ON ROME

88 B.C.

Uncle Marius seemed to be in a continual state of rage these days. Old Marius had won an important victory for Rome in the war with the Italian rebels, and he wasn't getting the credit he thought he deserved. Once again, L. Cornelius Sulla was receiving all the glory. Sulla was so popular in Rome that he was elected consul, in spite of all Marius and his supporters could do to prevent it. Gratus the carriage-maker did his bit with a sign on his wall: MARIUS, FATHER OF OUR COUNTRY.

Just as Rome seemed to sigh with relief that the Italian rebellion was under control, couriers brought bad news from the East. Gaius heard it first from a town crier, on his way home across the city from the Field of Mars. Usually a crier would tease his audience with a bit of information, wait for some coins to drop into his hat, and then tell more. But this crier poured his story out as if he couldn't hold it in.

"Citizens, Mithridates's rebels have butchered *eighty thousand* Roman citizens in Asia Minor!"

"Asia Minor! That could have been Father," said Gaius to Myro. It was only three years ago that Gaius Caesar the Elder had been governor of the province of Asia Minor.

The crier continued, "Not just soldiers, or tax collectors. They slaughtered merchants, students, even travelers who just came to see the sights. Even children!"

"Who is this Mithridates, young master?" asked Myro.

"I think he's king of Pontus. That's a land on the Black Sea, near Asia Minor."

That afternoon the Senate held an emergency

meeting. Gaius begged his father to let him come, and he was allowed to join other senators' sons near the door of the Senate hall. Gaius's father took his seat in the third row of one side, next to a senator named Lucius Cornelius Cinna. Uncle Marius, along with Uncle Sextus, Cousin Lucius, and other former consuls, sat in the front row. Most of the three hundred senators were present, all with grim faces.

Consul Sulla stepped down from his dais to address the Senate. He laid out the bad news: Thousands of Romans (although perhaps not eighty thousand) had been killed by rebels in Asia Minor, incited by Mithridates of Pontus. Worse, Mithridates had sailed his fleet across the Aegean Sea to Athens, and the Greek city welcomed him like a liberator.

"He thinks he's a second Alexander the Great," shouted a senator. "He'll take over Asia Minor, then Greece—then, who knows?"

One after another, senators took the floor to give impassioned speeches. "The Senate and the People of Rome must crush this monster!" "Tear the ungrateful city of Athens to the ground!" One speaker quoted the end of Cato the Censor's famous speech about Carthage, only changing it to, "Mithridates must be destroyed."

After all the speeches, the Senate voted to send Sulla to Asia Minor with an army. Gaius saw Uncle Marius scowl at this.

When the meeting was over, Gaius joined his father and uncles and their friends, including Cinna, on the steps of the Senate building. Uncle Marius was saying, "Can you believe that vote? I'm the general who knows how to squelch a rebellion." He jerked a thumb toward his barrel chest. "Why don't they send *me*?"

Gaius was worried. Didn't Uncle Marius really know the answer? In the first place, Sulla was consul. It was customary to send a consul to command the army. Besides—Old Marius would turn seventy next year. He was one of the oldest men in the Senate. Looking from face to face, Gaius saw his thoughts reflected in the cautious expressions of his father and his other uncles.

But Cinna barely hesitated before imitating Marius's scowl. "Yes, why don't they send you, General? You'd have Mithridates in chains before he could scurry back to Pontus!"

Soon after the emergency Senate meeting, King Nicomedes of Bithynia, a country between Pontus and the province of Asia Minor, journeyed to Rome. He came to beg the Romans for help against Mithridates. As was customary for a petitioner, he appeared in the Forum dressed in rags, with ashes on his head. But later, Gaius saw him at a reception at Uncle Sextus's house. The rags and ashes were gone, and Nicomedes was dressed in robes embroidered with threads of gold and studded with jewels. In a room full of men in plain togas, he stood out like a peacock among ducks.

"If a Roman senator appeared in such frippery," sniffed Uncle Cotta, "the Censor would throw him out of the Senate." Yes, thought Gaius—but still, Nicomedes's clothes were glorious.

The Roman army gathered outside the city, on the Appian Way. Towns all over Italy contributed troops to fight the menace in the East. Meanwhile, Old Marius seemed to have something up his sleeve. When Gaius saw him in the Forum or at family gatherings, he had an excited gleam in his eye. He once clapped a hand on Gaius's shoulder and said, "Speed and surprise, my boy!"

In fact, before Sulla could leave Rome with the army, Marius used all his political clout to defy the Senate. With the help of a tribune, Sulpicius Rufus, he went to the people's Assembly. Sulpicius persuaded the Assembly to take away Sulla's command of the war with Mithridates and replace him with old Marius.

"This is madness!" exclaimed Aurelia when she heard. "Sulla won't stand for it."

Sure enough, Sulla fled to the army waiting for him outside the city. The troops begged

Sulla to stay on as their commander. "Sulla Felix!" they chanted worshipfully. "Lucky Sulla!"

A few days later in the Forum, Gaius and his father listened to the officials who'd gone out to try to argue with Sulla. "We were lucky to escape with our lives. His officers tore off our togas and chased us back down the highway." They still looked shaken. "Sulla refused outright to turn over his command. And not only that. Do you know what he told us? He said, 'I am coming to free Rome from her tyrants.'"

Even the senators who favored Sulla looked shocked. "He's *coming*?" repeated Uncle Cotta. "With the army? A Roman general, marching on the city he has sworn before Jupiter and Mars to protect?"

"Sacrilege!" roared Marius. Never before, in all the centuries of Roman history, had a consul led his army against Rome itself. A general was not even allowed to set foot inside the city until he gave up his command.

The next morning, Gaius woke up before dawn. He often woke up early and lay in bed. Sometimes he entertained himself by reciting parts of the *Iliad*, or by imagining the warhorse he'd ride into his first battle. Sometimes he sorted out things in his mind, such as how the Caesars were connected to all the other patrician families in Rome.

But today, the eerie quiet outside reminded Gaius that this was not an ordinary day. Rome was usually noisy, even this early. Wagons rattled, making their first deliveries; herders called to their sheep and the sheep *baa*ed; slaves chattered as they drew water at the public fountains.

This morning, though, Rome seemed to be holding its breath. Here and there a rooster crowed, sounding loud and ignorant. Only chickens could be unaware of what was happening: The commander sworn to protect the city was leading his army against it.

Jumping up, Gaius roused Myro from his pallet in the hallway. "Help me climb up on the roof. I want to see what's going on." The slave grumbled, but he followed Gaius into the courtyard.

On the ridge of the tiled roof, Gaius crouched among pots of Jove's Beard, plants that were supposed to ward off lightning. Ignoring his cold, bare feet and the sharp November air, Gaius squinted toward the east. Against the growing light he could see the notched top of the Esquiline Gate, the entrance to the Subura section of Rome.

Then trumpets rang out from beyond the gate. Gaius knew what those notes meant: "Charge!" A phrase came into his head: *Speed and surprise.*

In the street below, boots tramped over the paving stones. Gaius looked down at armed men streaming past the Caesars' doorway. He thought he recognized some of Tribune Sulpicius's bodyguards. They were heading uphill and east, toward the Esquiline Gate.

"What do you see, Gaius?" His mother was out of bed, too, pulling a shawl around her shoulders. Before he could answer, his father joined her in the courtyard. "Come down," he shouted. "At once!" he added, as Gaius lingered for one more look.

There was no disobeying a direct order from his father, so Gaius backed down the roof tiles on his hands and knees and lowered himself onto Myro's waiting shoulders.

"That must be Sulpicius's men out there, going to fight Sulla," he panted, pointing in the direction of the street. "And some others who looked more like gladiators than—"

His father interrupted him with a cuff on the head. "That was a foolhardy thing to do. What if they started using the catapults? How many sons and heirs do you think I have?" Turning to Myro, he gave him a cuff too.

Holding his smarting ear, Gaius stared at his father. He'd never seen him like this. It was normal for a Roman father to punish a disobedient son with a spanking or switching, but Gaius's father had never hit him in anger.

By this time the whole household was

crowded into the little courtyard. They looked
at Gaius Caesar the Elder, waiting for him to
decide what to do. "We can't stay here," said
Aurelia.

"Should we pack for the country, master?"
asked the valet.

"We'll go to Marius's house," said Gaius's
father, more loudly than he needed to. "Palatine Hill will be well protected."

Dressing hastily, the family grabbed a few
valuables and left the house. Gaius tucked a
scroll, a book of Greek plays he'd borrowed
from Uncle Cotta, inside his tunic. At Aurelia's
orders the slaves carried out the household
shrine, containing the masks of the ancestors.

The Subura Way, the main street of the dis-
trict, was crowded with people running this
way and that. There was no possibility of getting a litter, so the Caesars as well as their
slaves trudged through the streets and up the
slopes of Palatine Hill to Uncle Marius's.

The doorkeeper didn't want to let anyone
in, but finally Aunt Julia greeted them in the

atrium with a white face. "Praise Jupiter you're here, Gaius," she said to her brother. "Marius is on his way to Africa. Young Marius left just an hour ago, hidden in a wagon. Sulla has sworn to have their heads."

Marius's house didn't seem so well protected, after all. The Caesars walked on around the hill to Aurelia's brother's house. All that day, Gaius and his father and Uncle Cotta watched the battle from the highest point of Palatine Hill. They could see the struggle moving slowly across the Subura, marked by burning tenement buildings. Columns of black smoke rose into the sky as if the Subura were offering sacrifices to Mars.

The fighting went on overnight, but before morning, Sulla's men had won. A messenger came to Uncle Cotta's door with a notice from Consul Sulla: All senators loyal to the Republic were summoned to the Forum at once. "I had better go," said Gaius's father. He borrowed a toga from his brother-in-law.

Gaius expected to go to the Senate with his

father and uncle, but Gaius Caesar the Elder ordered him to stay with his mother. "If something happens to me, she will need you."

Nothing "happened" to Gaius's father, but he returned home looking grim. "Sulla forced us all to swear loyalty to him," he said as he changed his outdoor shoes for sandals. "He declared all of Tribune Sulpicius's laws invalid, including of course the one to give Italians and freedmen full voting rights." He added in a lower voice, "Sulpicius's head was on the Rostra."

"And Marius?" asked Aurelia.

Gaius Caesar the Elder shook his head. "I think he got away. If Sulla had had his head, he certainly would have displayed it."

The next morning the Caesars moved back to the Subura. The stale smoke hanging in the air made their eyes water. On the way they passed the charred wrecks of tenements, where former tenants were poking through the blackened rubble. But the Caesars' own house was unharmed. Aurelia set the slaves to cleaning up the layer of ashes in the atrium.

Feeling restless, Gaius slipped out to walk around the neighborhood. As he passed by Gratus the carriage-maker's shop, Gaius noticed something different about the wall. The sign MARIUS, FATHER OF OUR COUNTRY had been painted over. That is, MARIUS had been blotted out with white paint. In its place, new black letters proclaimed SULLA as FATHER OF OUR COUNTRY.

Suddenly furious, Gaius pounded on the solid wooden gate. "Citizen Gratus!" No one answered. Gaius pounded again, surprised at his own force. "Citizen Gratus!"

Finally a tiny window opened high in the door, and an eye appeared. "What's the matter?" asked the carriage-maker.

"False friend! Coward! How dare you paint out Uncle Marius's name!" demanded Gaius. "After all the gifts we've given you!"

"Oh, I'm a coward, am I?" Gratus gave a short laugh. "And where *is* your brave uncle Marius? Will he run back from Africa to protect me from Sulla's soldiers?"

Gaius didn't know what to say, although he still felt like pounding on something.

Gratus opened the door. His face was grimy with ashes, making the whites of his eyes stand out. "Look, young Caesar, I always did everything your family asked me to. I earned those gifts. And, frankly, if everything was equal, I'd just as soon leave MARIUS painted on my wall. But I'm only a humble citizen, trying to keep my shop from being burned down and my family from being slaughtered. To me and the baker and the tavern keeper"—he gestured down the street—"living in the city with Marius and Sulla is like living in a pen with two fighting bulls. We just try to stay out of their way."

CHAPTER 5
A BRIDE FOR GAIUS

87 B.C.

Sulla was at the top of the heap for the moment, but it seemed he wouldn't take revenge against the supporters of Marius as long as they kept quiet. In the Senate, even Gaius's father went along with the vote to outlaw Marius. He came home from the Forum in a bad mood that day. Aurelia sat up talking with her husband long into the night. From his bedroom, Gaius heard his father's angry voice: "Forced to vote against my patron! It's shameful."

His mother's voice was quiet and firm: "It was foolish of Marius, the position he put his people in. You couldn't help him by making Sulla angry with you now." She added, "If we can just lie low for a while, Cotta will put in a good word for us with Sulla."

Word got around that Old Marius had safely reached Africa, where many of his former troops were settled. Together with young Marius, he remained in Africa and waited for the right time. Meanwhile, the Marian faction was hopeful. Lucius Cornelius Cinna, an enemy of Sulla, had been elected consul for next year.

Right after the election that summer, Cinna gave a celebration party, and the Caesars were invited. For a while Gaius stayed with the men in the colonnade, listening to them rehash how they'd won the election. Then the sound of soft chords drew Gaius into the garden. In the far corner, a group was listening to a girl playing the cithara. An elderly, stern-looking woman beside her gave Gaius a fishy stare, but he gave her a disarming smile as he sat down.

There was something about this girl: Was it the way her slender fingers plucked the strings, or the subtle expressions coming and going over her face? She was singing a sad song, and her brown eyes were sad. But for an instant her eyes met Gaius's eyes, and a dimple showed in her cheek. Then a difficult run of notes took all her attention, and she seemed to be lost in the music.

Gaius nudged the boy next to him on the bench. "Who is that?"

"Don't you know?" the other boy asked. "That's Cinna's daughter, Cornelia."

One day that autumn, the Caesar family council gathered for midafternoon dinner at Uncle Sextus's house. Gaius's father brought him along to the council for the first time. "You might as well come—some of this concerns you," said Gaius Caesar the Elder. "Besides, Sextus doesn't want any slaves listening in. You can pour the wine."

Gaius was eager to sit in on the family council. He already had an idea, from catching bits of conversations between his mother and his father, of what would be covered. Aurelia had had suggestions on each topic, but she was especially firm about the one concerning Gaius.

At the meeting, most of the discussion was about Sulla. He now planned to leave for the East after the first of the year. Sulla knew he still had enemies in Rome, but Mithridates could not be allowed to overrun the eastern provinces any longer.

Uncle Sextus was surprised that Sulla trusted Cinna and the other new consul enough to leave them in charge of Rome. "Cinna will call Marius back before you can say 'thunderbolt.' We need to decide where we stand."

"We stand on a shaky bridge, Brother," said Gaius's father. "Old Marius is . . . not quite the man he used to be."

"No, but many of the common people still worship him. And it seems he can bring an army from Africa—all his veterans and their sons. With Cinna in charge to steady him, it'll be all right."

"Naturally we have to support our patron," Gaius Caesar the Elder said heavily. "But Sulla will return, sooner or later, and then . . ."

"Maybe not," Lucius Caesar put in. "Maybe he'll die in battle, and never return from Asia Minor."

The men's sober faces brightened at the thought. But then one of Gaius's older cousins spoke up. "I wouldn't count on that. He's protected by Venus Fortuna." There were murmurs of agreement and nodding of heads, and worried looks again.

Nothing was decided on that subject, except that the Caesar family would not take part in any actions to outrage Sulla's supporters. No defacing of his public statues, for instance.

Toward the end of the meeting, Gaius's father cleared his throat. "On another subject, brothers: As you know, my son is approaching the age of manhood. For his political career, he'll need more money than I can provide."

"Have you thought of the Cossetuians clan?" asked one of Gaius's great-uncles. "They have a girl available to be betrothed. The family is lower-class nobility, but they're rich. Very solid money: Spanish mines and Sicilian granaries."

The council discussed the pros and cons of two other possible brides for Gaius. "Will he really need all that money?" asked Cousin Lucius. "He's a bright boy, but it's not as though we expect him to conquer the world."

The men looked at Gaius, perched on a stool next to the wine table. He looked down modestly, holding back a smile as his father repeated his mother's words: "We feel—I feel—with all due humility, that my son will need that much money, and more, if he is to accomplish all that he can." The discussion went on for a little while after that, but Aurelia's opinion won out.

Next month, Gaius met his intended bride for the first time, to exchange the usual betrothal rings. Her name was Cossutia, of course, since a girl was always named for her clan. Afterward, he remarked to Aurelia, "Mother, Cossutia is pretty enough, but I don't think she's very bright. She just sat there and giggled at everything I said."

"Yes, I know." Aurelia sighed and smiled. "Don't complain—I'm the one who'll be stuck at home with a silly daughter-in-law while you'll go off to the Forum every day. Anyway, your marriage won't take place for a few years yet."

One day the following spring, Aurelia asked Gaius to go with her to a play that was showing in the Forum. It was a comedy, a farce by Plautus. "It'll be amusing," said Aurelia. "Also, the Head Vestal will be there, and I'll present you. Vestals can be powerful allies. If the Head Vestal likes you, she can help you a great deal."

Gaius had seen the Vestal Virgins in processions and at ceremonies, but he'd never had a chance to talk to one. The priestesses of Vesta didn't talk to just anyone—they were special, set aside. They had to take a vow never to marry, and they lived by themselves in the House of the Vestals, next to the Temple of Vesta on the Sacred Way.

Before Gaius and his mother left for the Forum, she made him change his tunic. There was only one little stain on the hem, but Aurelia insisted. As the valet redraped Gaius's toga, his mother explained, "You understand why dressing properly is important, don't you? It shows that you respect the person to whom you present yourself. And even if no one notices your clothes, you will respect yourself. Your dignity will show."

In the Forum, rows of benches for the audience had been set up in an open space. Chairs in front were marked off for really important people: CONSUL, PRAETOR, AEDILE, VESTAL.

The next few rows—still good seats—were

roped off for patricians, like the Caesars. Aurelia sent a slave to save seats while she and Gaius waited for the Vestals. Looking around the audience, Gaius noticed a familiar young man with a long neck. "There's Marcus Cicero, Mother."

"Oh, yes." Aurelia raised a hand in greeting. "He's with that Greek—a philosopher, by the looks of him. That must be Philo of Larisa."

Shortly before the play began, four women dressed all in white swept into the Forum. There were always six Vestals, but two were girls too young to go out in public. Aurelia bowed before the oldest Vestal and kissed her hand. "Reverend Maiden, I am glad to see you looking so well."

The Head Vestal nodded graciously. "Aurelia, greetings. How are your daughters? And this must be Gaius Julius Caesar the Younger."

"Yes, may I present my son?" Aurelia motioned Gaius to step forward. He also bowed and kissed the Head Vestal's blue-veined hand.

The priestess's face under her white shawl

was lined, but her eyes were penetrating. "I have heard good things about you, young Caesar. I hope you will continue to be a credit to the ancient and noble Julius clan and to the highest ideals of Rome."

Gaius and his mother bowed again, murmuring thanks. An attendant arranged cushions in the Head Vestal's chair, and the priestess settled herself.

As Gaius followed his mother toward their row, he heard the Head Vestal say to the priestess beside her, "What a charming lad!"

Aurelia had heard, too, and she turned to give Gaius a secret smile. "You see? That was well worth doing. You never know when you might need a Vestal on your side. Consuls and praetors, aediles and tribunes may come and go, but Vestals hold their office for life."

"Do you think she's really heard good things about me?" asked Gaius.

Aurelia shrugged. "Even if she was just being polite, the Head Vestal will remember you now." They reached the row where their slave had spread out a mat on the bench for them. Marcus Cicero, in the next row back, stood to greet Aurelia and Caesar.

"I thought you were much too serious a young man to watch a silly comedy," Aurelia teased him.

Cicero turned pink. "You're mistaken, ma'am. I appreciate all kinds of theater. You see, I believe that success in politics requires an understanding of the elements of drama: writing, acting, staging."

"Ah," said Aurelia. "So politics can be either a comedy or a tragedy? How true!" She went on: "I hear that the officials this year are stingy with money for the plays. I suppose we can't expect much of a show."

"Isn't it true, ma'am—you get what you pay for," agreed Cicero.

"Politicians get what they pay for too," Aurelia said tartly. "These officials won't win many votes if they skimp on the public works."

"Listen, the play's starting," said Gaius.

In front of the stage, the musicians began

to play a lively tune on their flutes. The audience settled down, and the narrator stepped through the center door. The door came away from the set and almost fell on him, but he managed to catch it. "See, I told you they were stingy with the theater money," whispered Aurelia.

But the narrator turned the accident into a joke, pretending extreme surprise. The idiotically smiling expression on his mask went well with his gestures as he examined the door from every angle. The audience laughed harder and harder until a stagehand appeared and took the door away. "At least they paid for good actors," Gaius whispered back.

"Yes, that was the test of a skilled performer," said Aurelia. "He kept cool, he acted as if he *meant* the door to come off in his hand—and he turned it into an advantage."

Although Sulla wasn't happy about Cinna's election as consul, he did nothing to stop him from taking office in January. Not that Sulla exactly trusted Cinna—he ordered the new consul to swear a solemn oath that he would uphold all of Sulla's new laws, including the death warrant for Marius.

"Cinna won't honor his vow, once Sulla and the army are out of Italy," said Sextus Caesar afterward. "I heard him say the gods would not mind if someone broke a *forced* vow."

Gaius wasn't that impressed with Consul Cinna, but he couldn't forget his young daughter Cornelia. Now and then he caught a glimpse of her at some function or other, always accompanied by the same fish-eyed chaperone. He once thought Cornelia almost smiled at him.

In the early spring, when the sea-lanes were safe for shipping, Sulla marched his army to the eastern port of Brundisium. A few days later, a courier galloped up the Appian Way to Rome and informed Consul Cinna that General Sulla was safely on his way across the Adriatic Sea to fight Mithridates. Within hours, Cinna had dispatched another courier across the Mediterranean toward Africa. Old Marius was waiting for this news, and he and his army took ship for Italy.

Consul Cinna had also raised troops, and now he urged the Senate to lift the ban on Marius. The Senate dithered and debated. On the one hand, Sulla had acted illegally in the first place when he entered Rome with an army. On the other hand, Marius was freeing slaves in southern Italy and enlisting them in his army. Maybe it was all right to free one well-behaved slave, now and then. But to free hundreds at a time *and* give them weapons— that was madness!

The Senate finally agreed to allow Marius to return to Rome as long as he promised not to take revenge on his enemies.

Gaius's father went around looking worried, but Gaius was caught up in the fever that ran through the city. He had hated it when Sulla was running Rome. Marius might be almost seventy, but he wasn't too old, it seemed, to lead an army to victory.

The next day a crowd of commoners paraded down the Subura's main street, shouting, "Hail, Marius!" Gaius ran out and joined them. "Hail, Marius!" he chanted. "Marius the Victor!" It was like a holiday, only more exciting. It must be, Gaius imagined, the way it felt to go into battle.

As the crowd jostled past the carriage-maker's shop, Gaius noticed Gratus out in front, working on a wheel. "Citizen Gratus, did you hear?"

"Hello, there, young Gaius Caesar."

"Did you hear? Marius is back from Africa! He'll be here any day!"

Gaius expected thc carriage-maker to cheer, but Gratus only nodded. "So. Venus Fortuna spins her wheel again." He demonstrated with a spin of the carriage wheel. "Up one day, down the next."

"But this is *good* fortune!" exclaimed Gaius. "Marius is for the common people."

Gratus looked up and moved his head from

side to side, as if weighing the pros and cons. "Good fortune for Marius and his family, no doubt. As for whether Marius's good fortune is good fortune for Rome . . ." He shrugged.

CHAPTER 6

GAIUS IS A MAN

87–85 B.C.

When Marius and his army reached Rome, he cast aside all promises. The soldiers went on a rampage, slaughtering all the senators who had ever given Marius the slightest offense. Marius's freed gladiators were the worst. They looted and burned; they killed anyone in their path.

On the way to the Forum for the first Senate meeting after Marius's return, Gaius's father kept shaking his head. "Cinna was supposed to keep Marius and his attack dogs under control," he muttered. "True, it's reasonable that Cinna would kill Sulla's hard-core supporters. But to slaughter Marcus Antonius the Orator!"

Marcus Antonius was one of the most respected patricians in Rome.

At the west end of the Forum, past the Temple of Vesta, posters showing Marius's old victories were displayed. Farther along, Gaius and his father joined Cousin Lucius and his retinue. "Merula is dead," Lucius Caesar told them abruptly.

"Merula, high priest of Jupiter?" asked Gaius Caesar the Elder. "Marius killed the high priest of Jupiter?"

"No. Merula didn't give them the chance. He slit his own wrists right in the temple— blood all over the god's statue." Lucius Caesar shuddered. "He did it to place a terrible curse on Jupiter's city so that Marius couldn't enjoy his victory."

The Caesars and their attendants worked their way down the crowded Forum to the Rostra. Marius was already standing on the speaker's platform, waving to a cheering throng. Old as he was, Marius still made an impressive figure in his crested helmet and his military breastplate and boots. His red general's cape billowed in the spring breeze.

Young Marius, standing behind his father, also wore military garb. All around the platform hulking men in armor, swords by their sides, kept a distance between the speaker and the public.

Cousin Lucius said in a low voice, "I see the Old Man brought his runaway slave bodyguards along."

"If you start turning slaves into soldiers," answered Gaius's father, "what's to stop them from cutting off *all* of our heads?"

Behind Marius, the heads of his enemies were displayed on poles. Gaius thought he recognized one of them. "Is that Publius Crassus, Father?"

"Yes." Gaius's father looked at the head, swallowed, and looked away. "So Marius mowed down Crassus, a former consul, without a trial."

"And he was peaceably on his way into exile, they say," said Cousin Lucius. "His older son, too. The younger son, Marcus Crassus, may have escaped."

Gaius remembered the young man, whom he'd seen at Julia Minor's wedding, lounging on a cushioned dining couch. Now Marcus Crassus was running for his life.

What would Gratus the carriage-maker say, Gaius wondered, when he heard about Merula's death? *Blood all over the god's statue.* Gaius supposed the College of Pontiffs would order a ritual cleansing ceremony for the Temple of Jupiter, although that wouldn't really reassure the superstitious Romans.

Gaius also wondered who would be appointed to replace the dead priest. Although the high priest of Jupiter was given great respect, Gaius thought he lived an unappealing life. The high priest was forbidden to ride a horse or to see a soldier. When he went out in public, he had to wear an odd, pointed fur cap.

Around the Rostra, the cheering went on and on. The crowd began to chant Old Marius's nickname: "Old Man! Old Man!"

Smiling, Marius lifted off his helmet and handed it to an aide.

Under cover of a new burst of cheers, Lucius Caesar remarked to Gaius's father, "The Old Man looks as bad as one of those cut-off heads."

Gaius thought so too. Marius had been "the Old Man," as his soldiers called him, ever since Gaius could remember. But that name had only meant he was weather-beaten and battle-scarred, and that the hair under his victor's laurel wreath was gray. Now, though, it wasn't only Marius's hair that was gray. His face, under its leathery tan, was also lacking in color.

"Did I ever tell you how I made it to Rome in time to win my first consulship?" Marius was talking to the crowd. "The conservative senators didn't want a man like me, a man of the people, to be consul!" Roars from the crowd. "They gave me exactly twelve days to travel all the way from Africa to Rome! Didn't I cross the sea in four days? Didn't I enter Rome, with all of you cheering me, just like today, in time to register for consul?" After each question, the crowd shouted their lungs out.

Gaius's father and his cousin didn't shout, and neither did he. Part of Gaius seemed to be standing apart, watching this old general and his mob, the way the gods were said to watch humans. Did they sometimes get disgusted, he wondered, and stop watching? If Rome's patron god, Jupiter, abandoned his city, any terrible thing could happen: fire, earthquake, flood, plague, invasion of the barbarians.

Marius joined Cinna as coconsul. The next Kalends of January, Marius and Cinna began another year as consuls. A consul was not supposed to hold the office for more than a year at a time, but no one objected. On January thirteenth, Marius died suddenly.

The Caesars put on black clothes for mourning and gathered to talk about the Old Man. "He was a true Roman hero," said Uncle Sextus, tears running down his cheeks.

"Yes," said Gaius's father through his own tears, "and if he'd only died ten years ago, it would have been better for all of us."

The day before the funeral, Gaius received a note and a scroll from Marcus Cicero. "My condolences on your illustrious uncle's death," Cicero wrote. "I composed this eulogy poem in his honor."

At Marius's funeral, the Forum was packed with mourners, throngs of common people as well as Marius's family and friends. Gaius saw gray-headed veterans sobbing as they passed by the litter with Marius's body. Young Marius gave a eulogy for his father, and Consul Cinna spoke too. "Citizens," said Cinna in his funeral oration, "all Rome mourns her father, Marius."

"Not *all* Rome—not Sulla's senators," muttered one of the uncles in Gaius's ear. "Cinna thinks he can hold on to power, but just wait until Sulla returns from the East."

That spring, Gaius Julius Caesar the Younger became a man. On the morning of March 17, the Feast of Liberalia, in the year that Lucius Cornelius Cinna and Gnaeus Papirius Carbo were consuls, Gaius dressed like a boy for the last time. He joined his family in the atrium, packed with relatives. An augur, a friend of the Caesars', was also present to read the omens and pronounce the day favorable for such an important ceremony.

Gaius Caesar the Elder said the prayers in front of the shrine. Gaius, removing his purple-bordered boy's toga, set it in front of the bronze figure of the *Lar*, the guardian of the household. He also took off his gold *bulla*, the amulet he'd worn since his naming-day, and laid it in the *lararium* cabinet.

Aurelia stepped forward with a new toga. "My son, I have spun and woven your man's toga with my own hands, with a Roman mother's devotion," she said formally. "Wear it with the honor and courage of a true man."

As Gaius stood with arms outstretched, the valet slave draped the plain white toga just so: over the left shoulder, around the back, folded, rolled, and over the left shoulder again. Aurelia signaled to the musicians, and the pipes and tambourines started up. Led by the augur, the men of the family processed out the front door and toward the Forum.

Along the Subura Way, shopkeepers and workers called out, "Congratulations, young Caesar! Good luck! May Jupiter smile on you!" They also called to his father, walking just behind Gaius: "Congratulations on your fine son, sir! May he always bring you honor!" Gaius Caesar the Elder's steward handed out coins.

Many boys like Gaius, self-conscious in their brand-new togas, streamed onto the Sacred Way. At a solemn pace they led their relatives the length of the Forum. The Forum was crowded as usual, but everyone, even noblemen, respectfully made way for the boys about to become men.

Like consuls on the first day of their term, the boys and their kin climbed the steep ramp up Capitoline Hill. At the northern summit, the highest point in the city of Rome, they waited for an omen. Their togas rippled in the stiff breeze blowing up the cliff. Sunshine came and went quickly as clouds scudded in front of the sun. A speck of a bird appeared and turned into a hawk, sailing past the cliff top on out-spread wings. "It flies from west to east," pronounced the augur. "That's a good omen, very good."

Then they proceeded to the temple. Each boy offered a sacrifice to the statue of Jupiter, who sat in the sanctuary brandishing his thunderbolts and eagle-topped staff. Gaius thought briefly of the high priest of Jupiter, who had killed himself in the temple.

Outside the temple, each of the men in the family stepped forward to greet Gaius man-to-man, with a formal embrace. Gaius felt like embracing the whole city of Rome—the whole world! He seemed to be filled with marvelous powers, as if he could see beyond the northern horizon to the Alps—to Gaul—across the ocean to the legendary Hebrides Islands. He would be as great a general as Uncle Marius, Gaius vowed. But he would never let the frenzy of Mars destroy his judgment.

Back down in the Forum, each boy registered with his tribe, because Romans voted by tribes. The Caesars belonged to the Julian clan, which belonged to the Fabian tribe. As the Fabian official directed, a scribe wrote down Gaius's voting name: Gaius Julius Caesar the Younger. "Welcome to our tribe, Citizen," the official told Gaius.

Late that afternoon, after the family celebration, Gaius Caesar the Elder took his son into the courtyard. He called a slave to bring wine, and they sipped it and watched the daylight fade. Gaius's father finally said, "You know that the high priest of Jupiter's seat is vacant."

Gaius gave his father a puzzled look. Why was he bringing this up? It wasn't a cheerful subject, considering how Merula had killed himself in the Temple of Jupiter.

"Consul Cinna thinks you're just the man," Gaius's father went on.

"Me!" exclaimed Gaius. "Not me!"

"You have all the qualifications," his father went on, looking across the courtyard at a slave lighting the lamps. "A good patrician family, a sharp mind, you carry yourself well in public, and so on."

"Father!" pleaded Gaius. "If I become the priest of Jupiter, I'll never have the chance to do anything else. I couldn't go into the army at all." *Let alone become a great general,* he added to himself. "I might as well become a Vestal Virgin!"

"Don't be silly," his father said sternly. "A youth can't be a Vestal."

It was no use being sarcastic with his literal-minded father. Gaius could see, in a way, why his father had agreed to this. Cinna *was* offering Gaius a position of honor. And one of Cinna's supporters needed to fill the role as soon as possible. The longer it went vacant, the more the Romans would worry about Jupiter deserting the city.

"Wouldn't I have to go through a long training?" Gaius asked desperately. "I thought they wanted to appoint a priest as soon as possible."

His father nodded. "Yes, yes, but it's even more important to appoint the right person. The Chief Pontiff feels it would be worthwhile to wait for you." As Gaius opened his mouth again, his father held up his hand. "Your duty to Rome is clear. There's nothing more to say about it."

Gaius's heart sank. So the powers in control of Rome expected him to serve as high priest of Jupiter. His life was mapped out for him. It wouldn't include a glorious career in politics or war. It wouldn't even include stepping outside the city limits.

The next morning, after his father had left for the Forum, Gaius went to Aurelia to plead. "Mother! Help me get out of this! Do you know that I can canter with both hands behind my back? But after I'm high priest of Jupiter, I'll never ride on a horse again. Never!"

"I know," said Aurelia. She sighed.

"And I'll never fight in a battle! I won't even be allowed to *watch* a battle. Or even to see someone *else's* triumphal parade." Gaius's tone was bitter.

"This isn't what I had in mind for you, either," said his mother quietly. "But what choice do we have if Cinna and his council want you as the high priest of Jupiter?"

Gaius didn't have an answer—except that he was determined not to give in to such a fate. He set off for the meeting of a youths' club, the Sons of Apollo, on the Field of Mars. But first, he stopped at the shopping arcade in the Forum and went into a perfumer's shop. He sniffed all the flasks of scent before choosing one of the most expensive.

"I don't have enough money with me, though," he said.

"I know your family, young Caesar," said the shopkeeper. "Bring the rest of the price tomorrow." Putting his head on one side, he smiled slyly. "So, you just put on your manly toga yesterday and now you're giving ladies perfume?"

Gaius grinned sheepishly, but he didn't explain that the shopkeeper misunderstood. Besides, Gaius didn't think he was too young to give ladies perfume. Women liked him; that was the truth of it. His mother and sisters and aunts liked him; the baker's wife liked him; the Head Vestal liked him; the tavern maids liked him.

Gaius carried the crystal flask, wrapped in a square of linen, through the Fontinal Gate. Outside the public baths, at the edge of the Field of Mars, there was a shrine to Venus. Venus wasn't only the goddess of love; she could also be the goddess of good luck and of victory in battle. The statue in this shrine showed her wearing a helmet and resting one hand on a shield.

Bowing, Gaius held the flask high. "Venus Fortuna, Venus the Victorious, my ancestress and protector." Pulling out the stopper, he poured the expensive perfume, all at once, onto the base of the statue. A cloud of scent billowed up, almost choking him.

At the meeting, the other youths teased Gaius about his sweet, sweet smell. He didn't care. He felt that he and the goddess had a special understanding.

One of the privileges of manhood was that Gaius could go to the public baths with his father. The baths weren't just for bathing; they were also for socializing. Every day the gathering of bathers was like a big, open party, with the most interesting people in Rome.

One day at the Flaminian Baths, for instance, Gaius joined a group of young noblemen. They were gathered around Posidonius, a philosopher and ambassador from Rhodes. Gaius dropped into the pool, treading water while he listened. Marcus Cicero was complimenting Posidonius on his recent speech to the

Senate. "You put it so well, Ambassador Posidonius, on Rome's mission to the world: to bring the rest of the world into harmony with the overarching order intended by Heaven— positively inspiring."

CHAPTER 7

EVERYTHING
CHANGES

85–84 B.C.

Now that Gaius was a man, he began seriously preparing for his political career. Uncle Sextus guided this part of his education. "Think about it, Nephew," said Uncle Sextus as Gaius climbed the steps of the Senate building with him for the first time. "These three hundred men—and you will be one of them in a few years—rule an empire of millions. It's an awesome responsibility." Uncle Sextus took his place in the front row, reserved for former consuls. Gaius and other patrician youths stood near the tall, bronze doors to listen.

As time went on, Gaius didn't hear anything from Consul Cinna about the post of high priest of Jupiter, and he didn't ask. He supposed that Cinna was obsessed with worry about Sulla. Sulla's army, after two years of fighting, had defeated Mithridates of Pontus. The news was announced in the Senate: Sulla had made a hasty treaty with Mithridates and was now on his way back to Rome.

An old senator complained, "Why, in the name of Roma Victorious, didn't Sulla execute Mithridates while he had the chance? It's outrageous making peace with that despicable, treacherous rabble-rouser."

Gaius thought it was obvious why Sulla had settled for an enormous amount of money—some 3,000 gold talents—and a fleet of seventy fully supplied ships. Armies were tremendously expensive. If Sulla paid his soldiers himself, he could count on their loyalty. If he waited for the Senate to vote funds for his army—well, his troops might find something better to do.

"The question isn't what Sulla should have done with Mithridates," growled young Marius. "The question is, what are we going to do with

Sulla? He marched on Rome once, and he'll do it again."

Gaius knew very well that the high priest of Jupiter couldn't have anything to do with the army. But since no one told him not to, Gaius reported to the Field of Mars regularly and trained for war with other youths. One morning late in the spring, the Field of Mars gave off a rich scent of trampled grass and earth. Myro helped Gaius put on his helmet and his mail tunic for sword drill.

"Men, pair off!" Postumus Rufus, the centurion in charge of training, motioned the youths to pick up their wooden blades. As the pairs practiced parries and thrusts, he strolled among them, barking advice: "Put your weight into the thrust! Pretend it's Mithridates's pretty face behind the visor!" Now and then he pushed a pair of youths apart and demonstrated the technique himself. Gaius noticed he didn't say anything about the battle they might be fighting next, against their fellow Romans.

After sword fighting until their arms ached, the young patricians ran races, wrestled, and threw javelins. They practiced mounting and dismounting their horses while fully armed. When practice was over, the youths dropped their weapons for the armory slaves to pick up and raced to the riverbank for a swim.

Gaius was as hot and sweaty as any of the trainees, but he lingered to talk to Rufus. "Centurion, were you with my uncle Marius at the Battle of Aquae Sextiae?"

Postumus Rufus looked at him, surprised. "Not many your age want to hear about Aquae Sextiae. Aye, I joined up with the Old Man. Why not? I couldn't make a living hanging around the Forum, that's for sure. And they said he was promoting men from the ranks. Which turned out to be true for yours truly." The centurion jabbed a thumb at his own chest. Then he stopped talking. "You don't want to hear about all this."

"Yes, I do," said Gaius. "Please go on."

So the centurion explained how different it

was, serving under General Marius. It used to be that each soldier had to furnish his own armor and weapons, but Marius bought his men shields and good Spanish-forged swords. On the trail, the Old Man saw to it that his troops had shelter and decent rations, and he sat down at their campfires and ate with them. Not only that—when the war was over, he rewarded each legionary with a farm.

"So we'd follow him anywhere," said the centurion, brandishing his spear. "If Marius ordered us to throw a pontoon bridge across the River Styx, march over it double-time, and conquer the underworld—why, we'd just do it."

Gaius's heart swelled as he listened. How would it feel to be a commander like Uncle Marius? To know that thousands of men would follow *him* to Hades and back?

A short while later, floating on his back in the river, Gaius wondered what kind of an officer his father was. He'd seen his father drilling soldiers on the Field of Mars, but not leading troops in an actual battle. At the moment,

Gaius Caesar the Elder was in the town of Pisa, northwest of Rome. Consul Cinna needed fresh troops to fight Sulla, and Gaius's father was in charge of recruiting soldiers in that region.

Back home that afternoon, Gaius called the scribe into the office to write a letter. The steward also came in with the household accounts, and Gaius looked over the figures while he dictated:

From Gaius Caesar the Younger, at Rome,
To his father at Pisa, greetings.

Gaius wondered how many recruits his father had managed to scrape together by now. As soon as Consul Cinna had a sizable force, he'd leave for Macedonia. Cinna wasn't well liked by soldiers, Gaius had heard. But Sulla's troops, puffed up with their victories and laden with booty, would naturally be very happy with their general.

Gaius, man of the house in his father's

absence, reported the news in his letter. Julia Minor was pregnant. . . .

"Young master." Gaius looked up from the accounts to see the doorkeeper at the entrance to the office. "Your uncle Sextus Caesar and cousin Lucius Caesar are here to see you, young master."

Puzzled, Gaius let the accounts scroll roll itself up as he rose from the table. Why were his uncles behaving so formally instead of just walking into the office? Waving to the scribe to put down his pen, Gaius hurried toward the atrium. "Call my mother," he told the slave.

Uncle Sextus and Cousin Lucius embraced Gaius. "Gaius Caesar," each one greeted him.

Why were his relatives calling him by his father's name? Gaius was just "Gaius" to them, and "Gaius Caesar the *Younger*" to everyone else.

Uncle Sextus held out his hand to Aurelia, appearing beside Gaius. "Sister-in-law, greetings."

Gaius glanced at his mother. She looked as if

she was bracing for a blow. He took her other hand.

"We have bad news from Pisa," said Uncle Sextus.

Then Gaius knew: His father was dead.

Gaius Caesar the Elder had not died by violence, like so many others. A few days ago, while getting dressed, he had died of a stroke.

To show that the Caesar household was mourning, a cypress bough was hung outside the door. The Caesars put on black clothes. Gaius's father's body was brought home from Pisa and laid out in the Caesars' atrium. Gaius tried to take in the idea that his father's life was over.

Gaius had known, of course, that his father would die sometime. Uncle Marius, dying at the age of seventy, had lived an unusually long life. But Gaius had imagined that his father would die only on some distant day, after Gaius was launched on his political career.

First, Gaius would serve on some governor's

or general's staff, as young patrician men always did. Then he would begin practicing law in the Forum. Then he would serve in the provinces as a quaestor, assistant to the governor. Then he would join the ranks of senators, and he would be ready to run for a lower-level political office. *Then,* perhaps, would it seem natural for his father to die.

On the day of the funeral, Gaius's father's body was dressed in his praetor's robes and laid on an open bier, decked with wreaths and flowers. Hired actors wore the masks of the Caesar ancestors in a procession to the Forum, while musicians played flutes and drums. Relatives from both sides of the family followed the bier. At the head of the train, Gaius and his father's brother rode in a chariot.

In the Forum, Gaius's uncle Sextus spoke about his brother: an honorable Roman citizen of ancient lineage, a good father to his children, dutiful servant to the Republic, a just governor of Asia Minor, etc.

Gaius listened respectfully. But privately he thought, *My father's life is over, and this is all it adds up to. This is the end of his chance to do something glorious, something to be remembered.*

The fact was, Gaius's father hadn't done anything memorable. There would be no statues in the Forum to Gaius Julius Caesar the Elder. No coins with his likeness would be minted. No plays or poems would be written about his life, to be recited at banquets in years to come. His bones would be laid to rest in the Julian tomb outside the city, and that would be that.

What would be the sum of Gaius's own life? Nothing much, if he became the high priest of Jupiter. He could never distinguish himself in politics or on the battlefield. Smothering panic closed down on Gaius as if he himself were the one to be shut in a tomb.

Noticing a worried look from his mother, Gaius forced a serene expression onto his face. A true Roman did not panic, especially in public.

Gaius would stay calm—but he would *not* give in to an ordinary destiny.

After the funeral, Gaius Caesar was the head of his family. Every morning he recited the prayers to the household gods. On the Kalends, the first of the month, he was the one who sacrificed the pig. Clients now followed *him* to the Forum or waited outside *his* door to ask for favors.

Gaius Caesar continued to attend Senate meetings, to listen in on debates, and to practice military skills on the Field of Mars. But now he also had to show up regularly at the College of Pontiffs for his training as high priest of Jupiter. The more he learned about the office, the more he felt like he was being squeezed into a tiny space.

However, there was one rule about the high priest of Jupiter that didn't bother Gaius Caesar: His wife would have to be a patrician. So he couldn't marry Cossutia, whose family was equestrian, the lower nobility. But Gaius

Caesar didn't point this out to anyone, because it seemed like one step closer to taking office as high priest. Every now and then he paid a dutiful visit to his betrothed.

If Gaius Caesar had only a year or so to live the way he liked, he was determined to cram everything into it. He went daily to the public baths to work out in the exercise yard, exchange news, and join in debates. He attended chariot races at the Circus Maximus and plays in the Forum.

Gaius Caesar's young friends gave many parties, and he went to all of them. He gave parties, too, serving his guests the most expensive foods and wines, although he himself never ate or drank too much. Caesar and his friends went shopping in the Forum, coming home with togas of the softest weave, imported scent, crates of fine wine, or sometimes a slave. Caesar bought a new valet, Tithonus, who spent hours on his master's grooming.

Now Caesar was old enough for a tutor, and he studied with Gnipho of Alexandria. Gnipho had Caesar practice projecting his voice, matching his tones and gestures to his subject, and collecting quotations that might come in handy in a debate. Some days Caesar would join Gnipho and a few other students to take turns reciting for one another.

Often Gnipho would say, "You might find so-and-so interesting," and hand Gaius Caesar a scroll. Caesar usually did find it interesting, whether the book was about travels, science, or philosophy. One of the most exciting books to him was by the philosopher Epicurius.

The morning after reading this book, Caesar appeared at Gnipho's door eager to discuss Epicurius's ideas. He found Gnipho in the columned courtyard with Marcus Cicero and an older man. Cicero introduced his companion, a Greek scholar of philosophy named Diodotus. Caesar gathered that Cicero had taken the man into his household; many wealthy Romans had a live-in poet or philosopher.

Within a few minutes, the three of them were arguing about the nature of things while

Gnipho put in a word here and there. "Isn't it true, what Epicurius says?" asked Caesar. "Everything's changing, all the time! Nothing stays still. A plant grows, or it shrivels. The moon waxes and wanes. A general conquers a city and rewrites all the laws."

Diodotus smiled gently at Caesar. "Naturally it could seem, to a youth such as yourself, that change is the principle of the universe. But my dear Gaius Caesar, consider the unchanging verities that lie beneath the superficial changes you mention. For instance, the mild warmth of May *changes* to the heat of Quintilis—but we can always expect that change." Dabbing at his moist brow with the sleeve of his tunic, Diodotus gestured a slave with a fan to come closer. "Thus, as the Stoics understand, the change of the seasons is itself an eternal constant."

"But that's Epicurius's point, isn't it?" asked Caesar. "Change *is* the eternal constant. A baby is born changing, and he changes until he dies, an old man."

"Not Curio," joked Cicero, referring to a

well-known senator. "He'll always give his speeches as if he were standing in a rowboat." He held out one hand to an imaginary audience, bobbing and swaying. "Friends, citizens—"

Caesar laughed. "That's Curio to the life!" Diodotus, who didn't seem to have much sense of humor, droned on.

Listening to Diodotus with one ear, Caesar mused: Since everything was always changing, how could a man keep his balance? Caesar thought of the acrobats he'd seen performing in the public squares. Muscled like racehorses, they threw themselves into the air with enough power to kill themselves, or someone else. Yet they landed on their feet—even on one another's shoulders!—as lightly as butterflies.

It was all in their balance and timing, thought Caesar. They risked breaking their necks, and they did it so gracefully. That's what made the crowd gasp and cheer and drop coins in the acrobat's hat.

Caesar's mind leaped ahead to another question: Why had Marcus Cicero invited a bore like Diodotus to join his household? Cicero was an ambitious young man, so he must have chosen Diodotus to make a good impression on Roman senators. Most of them were stodgy conservatives; they liked to think that nothing really changed. That nothing *should* change.

Caesar smiled to himself. If he was going to add someone to his household, it would be an acrobat, not a philosopher.

One afternoon just before dinner, Gaius Caesar sat in the courtyard of his house, reading a friend's travel diary from Egypt. At the same time, he was composing an epic poem on the subject of the Roman hero Marcus Curtius. He heard Aurelia, who had been out, come in the front door.

His mother appeared in the courtyard entrance, handing her shawl to a slave. "Gaius, dear." She sat down on the bench opposite him. "How would you like to marry the most delightful, most suitable girl in the Republic?"

"What?" Caesar's mental pictures of adventures on the Nile River and of the heroic death of Curtius both evaporated, and he stared up at his mother. She couldn't be talking about the girl he was engaged to. "You don't mean Cossutia, do you?"

"Cossutia seemed like a good choice at the time. We were concerned about getting you enough money to launch your political career." Aurelia's eyes sparkled, like a child with a big secret. "But if you were the son-in-law of the first citizen of Rome, that would be worth any amount of money."

"The first citizen of Rome—"

"—is Lucius Cornelius Cinna." Aurelia beamed at him. "I mean his daughter, Cornelia."

"Mother!" Leaping to his feet, Caesar pulled Aurelia up and hugged her. "How did you do it?" He'd never mentioned his feelings for Cinna's daughter, but now he realized that his mother must have understood how he felt.

Aurelia held her son at arm's length, giving him a sly, sideways glance. "Why, whatever made you think I had anything to do with it? Well—perhaps I pointed out the obvious to Cinna. He has so many things on his mind. He wasn't considering the fact that, as high priest of Jupiter, you'll need a patrician wife. Furthermore, Cinna isn't completely secure in his power; he would be glad to be connected with our family."

The next day, Caesar received an invitation to Consul Cinna's offices. They agreed on the amount of Cornelia's dowry, the money that Cinna would give his daughter to bring to the marriage. The same day, Caesar sent a formal statement to Cossutia to break their engagement. And he bought another gold ring with clasped hands. Cinna consulted the augurs, and they found a favorable day for the wedding.

Some Roman weddings were very simple, and divorces could also be simple. But Caesar and Cornelia's wedding ceremony had to be the elaborate, traditional kind, called *confarreatio*. The high priest of Jupiter was required to be married this way. And, unlike other

Romans, he couldn't divorce easily.

On the morning of his wedding day, Caesar stood up in front of the assembled families and their important friends. Cornelia faced him in her bride's white gown and flame-colored veil. As the matron of honor joined their hands, Caesar whispered to Cornelia, "I am the luckiest man in Rome." She answered by squeezing his hand.

The wedding feast at Cinna's mansion went on for the rest of the day, beginning with platters of shucked oysters, sea urchins, and hardboiled quail eggs in lettuce cups. At nightfall, Caesar played his traditional part and pretended to tear Cornelia away from her mother's arms. Trying not to laugh, Cornelia pretended to cling to her mother. Caesar pulled his bride out the door and led her through the streets to his house, followed by a horde of musicians, slaves with torches, and singing wedding guests.

Outside the house in the Subura, where Gaius Caesar had grown up, they paused. Even with all the people around them, Caesar seemed to be in a place alone with Cornelia as he spoke the traditional words to her: "What is thy name?"

Cornelia answered, "Where thou art Gaius, I am Gaia." This meant that from now on, they were one person. As the wedding guests applauded, Caesar picked up his bride and carried her over the threshold.

Caesar felt lucky to have Cornelia for his wife, and the whole household shared in his good fortune. Aurelia was glad to have her daughter-in-law's company. Julia Minor came to visit more often. Even the Caesars' slaves, who weren't supposed to have an opinion about their masters, acted more cheerful and willing now.

But in spite of this great happiness in his private life, Gaius Caesar soon felt squeezed into a pen again. He wouldn't mind becoming a priest, he thought, if he could join the College of Pontiffs. Pontiffs, like Uncle Cotta, were priests, but they didn't actually perform ceremonies. A pontiff supervised the ceremonial priests like the high priest of Jupiter, and he received honor and power. But he didn't have to change his way of life.

Cinna now made frequent remarks about how important it was to have a fully trained, official high priest of Jupiter in place. Caesar knew that it *was* important; Romans got very uneasy if they felt that Jupiter, their patron god, wasn't being served in the proper way. Whether they were right or not, the commoners could cause serious trouble. One time, all the workers in Rome had simply stopped doing their jobs. Other times, they had rioted.

Finally, the College of Pontiffs set a date for Caesar's installation. Caesar Gaius felt like a fine young patrician bull being led to the sacrifice. He saw his chances to make a mark on the world dwindling away.

On his way to the Forum the next morning, Caesar took a detour to the shrine to Venus outside the city gate. His freedmen and slaves waited while he bowed before the statue of the goddess. Caesar didn't really believe in the gods anymore—at least not the gods as larger-than-life people sitting up in the sky. Still, he believed in some force larger than human beings. You could call it fate, or destiny—or Venus Fortuna.

"I vow a solemn and sacred vow," Caesar told Venus, "if you grant me the chance to win glory in this life, I will give you the honor."

The smile on Venus's lovely face seemed to deepen. He imagined her voice, low and sweet: *All right, Gaius Julius Caesar. You'll get your chance.*

As Caesar turned from the shrine, tremendous power seemed to surge through him. He felt like an acrobat flying through the air. At the same time, a second voice, quiet and sane like that of Gnipho of Alexandria, spoke in his head: *Be careful what you wish for.*

CHAPTER 8

THE DEATH LIST

83–82 B.C.

Consul Lucius Cornelius Cinna, Caesar's father-in-law, was dead. Murdered. Gaius heard the news in the Forum, from a cluster of senators huddling on the steps of the Temple of Castor. A military courier had just arrived from the east coast of Italy. Cinna's fleet had been battered by a storm in the Adriatic Sea, and several troopships were swamped. Among the soldiers who made it back to Italy, morale was very bad.

Still, how could Cinna have been murdered? "By his own men, in broad daylight," said Uncle Sextus Caesar grimly. "It couldn't be worse." There was a rumor that the soldiers were especially angry because their favorite officer, Pompey, was missing.

"Oh, those common soldiers love young Pompey," said Cousin Lucius sarcastically. "He combs his hair to look like Alexander the Great."

Gaius Caesar stood on the steps, hearing the same news over and over as newcomers joined the group. He had to go home and tell Cornelia that her father was dead. He shrank from the thought of his wife's tender face crumpling with grief. But this news was also a blow to Caesar and Aurelia and all the Caesar connections. As they put on black clothing and hung the cypress branch over their doorways, they would be mourning more than the loss of Cornelia's father. Consul Cinna had been their leader and protector.

It didn't help that Cousin Marius assumed he was the new Great Protector of the family. One evening in June, Gaius Caesar came home from a family council with a very bad feeling. "Marius is dead set on running for consul," he told Aurelia and Cornelia. "He's planning to raise an army and block Sulla when he lands at Brundisium. He wants me to join him as one of his officers."

"Don't do it," said Aurelia immediately. "Marius has no right to run for consul. He's never served as a praetor, and he's too young. The Senate won't support him. Even his mother realizes that. Your aunt Julia told me she *begged* Marius not to declare for consul."

"Yes, I know. Marius doesn't take her seriously—he was joking about 'women's fears' tonight." Caesar raised an eyebrow at his mother, one of the bravest people he knew. "But how can I refuse to serve with him?"

Cornelia spoke up. "You can't serve in the military at all. You're going to be the high priest of Jupiter."

Caesar looked from his wife to his mother. They both knew he wanted to get out of becoming the high priest of Jupiter, but Marius didn't know that. Aurelia nodded. "I thank the gods that we don't have all our eggs in one basket. She turned to Cornelia and said gently, "Forgive me for speaking bluntly at your time of grief for your father. Still, it's a good thing that my brother, as one of Sulla's officers, can put in a good word for us." So Caesar did not join his cousin Marius.

The month of June ended, with the weather in Rome even hotter and muggier than usual. On the sixth day of the month of Quintilis, shortly after Cousin Marius announced his candidacy for consul, there was a fierce thunderstorm. A lightning bolt struck the Temple of Jupiter on Capitoline Hill, and the temple burned.

Caesar climbed up the Capitoline the next morning with a few of his freedmen and slaves. A group of pontiffs, augurs, and builders was already there to inspect the damage. The temple roof had caved in, and the walls were shattered in many places. A canopy had been erected to shelter the exposed statue of Jupiter. "The temple will have to be rebuilt from the ground up," said the chief engineer.

The senior augur looked grim. "A disastrous omen for Rome. It couldn't be worse."

The pontiffs nodded. One of them, noticing Gaius Caesar, laid a sympathetic hand on his shoulder. "I'm afraid we'll have to put off your installation as high priest of Jupiter."

Caesar nodded soberly. "I understand." Inwardly, he could hardly contain his amazement. The disastrous omen for Rome was a lucky stroke for Gaius Caesar.

As Caesar was about to leave the hill, he spotted his tutor, Gnipho, among the people gathering to see the ruined temple. Gnipho looked more interested than worried. "Naturally, lightning over Rome would strike the Temple of Jupiter," he said to the youths with him. "Capitoline Hill is the highest point in the city. As Epicurius has observed, lightning will always strike the highest point."

Caesar shook his head at his tutor. "Sir, you'd better not say that out loud in the Forum. They'd stone you for blasphemy. The people are ready to stone young Marius, for that matter. On the way here I heard talk that Jupiter struck his own temple because Marius defied the Roman constitution by running for consul."

"Yes, your cousin Marius doesn't seem worried about either the wrath of Jupiter or the wrath of the Roman people," agreed Gnipho. "They say that while the temple was burning, his men pulled out fourteen thousand pounds of gold, not to mention the silver."

Later, the College of Pontiffs sent an official delegation to young Marius requesting that he hand the temple treasure over to the Vestal Virgins for safekeeping. But Marius ignored them. He wanted that money to fund his campaign for consul.

Cousin Marius won his election and he took office in January. Meanwhile, ominous bulletins reached Rome from the East as Sulla led his army toward the Adriatic Sea. The Senate sent envoys to Sulla to see if they could avoid civil war, but Sulla was determined to punish the Cinnans for their crimes against the Republic.

That summer, the Senate met to discuss some encouraging news: Sulla, off the coast of Italy now, was willing to make peace without punishing his enemies. Papirius Carbo, Cousin Marius's coconsul, presided over the meeting, but he had a hard time keeping order. The senators were as nervous, Gaius Caesar thought, as a flock of geese. They couldn't sit still, or keep silent.

"Romans, Senators." A respected old senator in the front row stood up, and the meeting grew quiet. "Sulla is our general, and he has defeated our enemy, Mithridates. Why shouldn't we come to terms with him?"

"We don't need to negotiate with that traitor," exclaimed Marius. "We have fifteen legions ready for battle. Sulla's soldiers have just finished a long, hard campaign. They won't want to fight another one, this time against fellow Romans."

"All the more reason to demand favorable terms from Sulla," retorted the old senator. "He'll have no choice."

Caesar noticed that his uncle Sextus said nothing, and his expression was blank. But Caesar was sure his uncle wasn't eager for civil war.

The Senate debated for hours. "On the one hand . . ." "On the other hand, with all due respect to my esteemed colleague, Senator . . ." *What is the matter with them?* wondered Caesar. *Are they stupid? Are they afraid?* In the end, Carbo and Marius forced the decision. With the consent of the Senate, their legions marched out to fight Sulla.

But Marius was wrong about Sulla's soldiers. They had great faith in their commander, Sulla the Lucky, and they were ready for more victories like the ones they'd won against Mithridates. They stood by him, and even more Romans joined Sulla's army.

Pompey, who had left Cinna's staff just before the consul was murdered, brought Sulla three legions. Pompey had raised the legions himself, Caesar noted, although he had no legal right to recruit soldiers. Marcus Crassus, too, emerged from hiding and joined Sulla's staff.

Battle after battle, Sulla fought his way north toward Rome that autumn. Carbo and Marius's legions melted away to join Sulla's. By November that year, Consul Carbo and Consul Marius were both dead. Carbo was captured and killed by Pompey. Marius, defeated by Sulla, killed himself.

Seizing Rome in a final battle, Sulla declared himself Dictator. He posted a list of his enemies in the Forum. This time he was determined to get rid of all of them. Any Roman could pick an "enemy of the Republic" from the list, hunt him down, and turn the head in for a bounty.

Caesar's aunt Julia and young Marius's widow, Licinia, weren't on the list, but they lost all their property: the mansion on Palatine Hill, the seaside villa, Licinia's dowry. Aurelia brought Aunt Julia and Licinia, with their personal maids, back home to the Caesars' modest house in the Subura. The house was quite crowded.

One day shortly afterward, an officer appeared at the Caesars' door with four guards and a summons. Caesar kept his voice steady as he read the summons aloud. "The Dictator Sulla requires Gaius Julius Caesar to appear before him at once." He looked up at his mother. Would she wail, as Aunt Julia had done for young Marius? But Aurelia held herself proudly, like a statue of a Roman matron. Cornelia's eyes were enormous in her pale face, but she followed Aurelia's example.

Caesar loved his two women more than he ever had before. In a calm, polite voice he told the officer, "Certainly, I will go with you. One moment while I change into suitable attire."

While the officer and his guards waited in

the atrium, Caesar dressed in his most formal clothing. Tithonus, his valet, handed him a tunic with fashionably long, fringed sleeves. Caesar belted the tunic loosely, in the elegantly careless look that was in style. He held out his arms while his valet draped his toga over his shoulders and adjusted the folds. Looking in a mirror of polished brass, Caesar watched Tithonus comb his hair in locks over his forehead.

Aurelia and Cornelia were waiting outside his room. Cornelia held her chin up, although it quivered. As Caesar kissed his mother, Aurelia said, "To be your mother has been the greatest blessing of my life."

"No man could have had a wiser or more devoted mother," answered Caesar, looking into her eyes. "Whatever happens, I will act so as to bring credit to my noble family." With a sudden grin, he added, "Don't worry, Mother. I'm not important enough to land on the death list."

Cornelia's lips trembled as she stepped forward to kiss him. "What is thy name?" Caesar whispered in her ear, quoting their wedding vows.

"Where thou art Gaius, I am Gaia," his young wife whispered back.

Caesar held her tightly for a moment, then turned away. With Sulla's officer beside him, he walked out the door at an unhurried pace. Maybe he would return to this house where he had lived for all of his eighteen years. Maybe he wouldn't.

The shops on the Subura Way were shuttered this morning, and hardly anyone was on the streets. The soldiers did not lay hands on Caesar, but two guards walked in front of him and two behind, while the officer kept close beside him. As they entered the Forum, Gaius Caesar noticed that Old Marius's trophies were missing from the upstairs arches of the Basilica Aemelia. So Sulla intended to rub out the very memory of Marius and all his deeds.

"The Senate voted to have a monument to Sulla the Lucky placed right there," the officer said to Caesar conversationally, pointing to a spot near the speaker's platform. "A gilded statue of the general on horseback. They've never given anyone that honor before."

The officer did not have to point out the severed heads on the Rostra. Gaius Caesar had always thought Cousin Marius was a bully and a braggart, but he felt a sick anger at seeing his body mutilated.

Sulla's headquarters was upstairs in the Basilica Aemelia. Two armed guards opened the doors for Caesar and his escort. Inside the reception room, Sulla sat in a carved chair beside a table. His secretary stood at a nearby writing stand, where a long scroll flowed over the top, almost all the way to the floor.

The officer saluted Sulla. "Here is Gaius Julius Caesar, sir."

As a boy, Caesar had seen Sulla in the Forum or on the Field of Mars many times.

But he hadn't seen him for years, especially at such close range. General Sulla had been handsome at one time, but now his skin was a pasty color, mottled with purple broken veins. There were bags under his pale blue eyes. When he wasn't in the field with his army, the gossips said, he liked to spend his evenings at wild, drunken parties.

With these thoughts going through his head, Caesar bowed to Sulla. Sulla looked him up and down, giving an amused snort. "Is that what fashionable young Romans are wearing these days?" He gestured at Caesar's fringed sleeves. "And have you forgotten how to tighten your belt?"

Caesar felt like a prisoner of war placed in the arena with a lion. He'd seen that happen. The lion had circled the man, playing with him, before pouncing.

"Don't misunderstand," Sulla went on. "I have the deepest respect for the Caesars and the Cottas, your parents' families. Of course the Caesars made a big mistake allying themselves with that lout Marius. But I won't hold that against *you*."

Caesar said nothing. He looked at the scroll on the secretary's writing stand. It was a list, a long, long list of names. He looked at the table, stacked with letter canisters. Some of them had been sealed with red wax and stamped with Sulla's seal. It was the same image as the gilded sculpture on the Capitoline Hill, the one that had enraged Uncle Marius years ago.

"The last few years have shown that we patricians have to stick together, hmm?" said Sulla. "Only the best men—men from old lines like the Cornelii and the Julii—should be consuls. If lesser men get into high positions, they commit dreadful crimes—like giving weapons to slaves and turning them loose on the city. As for the rabble, the People's Assembly, they should never be allowed to make important decisions."

Caesar felt his whole being shift into a state of high alertness. This man Sulla didn't simply want to kill Caesar; he wanted to force him to join Sulla's side.

"I'll get to the point," said Sulla, leaning forward on the arms of his chair. "The time has come for every Roman to decide whether he's an enemy of the Republic or a loyal citizen. I *could* assume you're an enemy, as nephew of that traitor old Marius, and as son-in-law of that traitor Cinna. But I'm an open-minded man." He paused as if he expected Caesar to agree.

Caesar bowed again, but still he was silent.

"Gaius Cotta tells me," Sulla continued, "that you show great promise." His eyes wandered from Caesar's carefully combed locks to his stylish boots. "He *didn't* mention that you'd show up dressed like a Greek prostitute." He winked, to show he was teasing. "However— I'm prepared to be generous with you if you'll prove your loyalty. If you divorce the traitor's daughter, you will be pardoned."

Divorce the traitor's daughter. Caesar hadn't expected this. His wife's face flashed before him, and he felt her soft arms around his neck. *Sacrifice Cornelia to this man?* he thought. *Sulla won't always be in power. Why should you sell out your beloved for him?*

"The General is merciful," said Caesar. "But—"

"I'm even willing to let you take office as high priest of Jupiter," interrupted Sulla, "although I've declared all of Cinna's decisions null and void."

"The General is most generous," said Caesar. He had the sense of balancing on the edge of a cliff. A misstep in one direction and he'd end up with his head on a stick. A misstep in the other direction and he would betray himself and everything he valued. Taking a breath, he continued in a steady voice. "It is with deep regret that I must refuse."

"Oh. Must you?" Sulla's mottled face seemed to flush a deeper purple, but he did not raise his voice. "So you think you're a better man than Pompey? He proved his loyalty in the first place by bringing me three legions. Then he brought me Carbo's head. Still, at a word from me, he divorced his wife and married my stepdaughter. Are you calling Pompey a coward?"

"No, General," said Caesar. To give himself courage, he imagined what Sulla's head would look like mounted on a pole. "I'm only saying that I'm not free to divorce my wife. I married Cornelia through the solemn rite of *confarrareo*. As you know, it is a grave matter to break such a marriage bond."

"I see." Sulla's pale blue eyes did not blink. "I didn't realize what a pious young man you are." Then, suddenly standing, Sulla clenched his right fist. Caesar thought the dictator was going to punch him, but Sulla only pushed his fist in front of Caesar's eyes. "Take a look at this ring." Sulla's heavy gold ring bore the image of a familiar goddess.

"Venus Fortuna," said Caesar.

"Correct," said Sulla. "Venus Fortuna. She

adores me. That's why they call me Sulla Felix, Sulla the Lucky. If you need to show your piety, this is the goddess to worship. It's no use fighting me. Venus Fortuna is on my side."

Caesar knew that almost everyone in Rome would agree with what Sulla had said. "Sulla Felix! Sulla Felix!" people chanted as he rode by. They said it to please him, of course, but they actually believed it too. Somehow, Caesar did not believe it.

"If you refuse," said Sulla, "you lose your darling wife's dowry, and of course her inheritance from her traitor father. I would think you'd be very sorry to lose all that money."

Caesar *was* sorry already—he'd had plans for that money. But, again, he said nothing.

"All right," said Sulla softly. He made a slight motion of his head to the officer standing near the door, and the man stepped forward to escort Caesar out. Sulla sank back into his chair, picked up a scroll, and began to read as if Caesar had already vanished.

Gaius Caesar walked out of Sulla's reception room with his heart pounding. He felt strangely triumphant. As he stepped between the sentries, he heard the dictator give his secretary an order, still without raising his voice: "Put him on the list."

CHAPTER 9

RUN FOR YOUR LIFE

81 B.C.

That same afternoon, Gaius Caesar found himself on horseback, trotting northward from Rome on the Flaminian Way. He wore a warm, long-sleeved tunic, a hooded traveling cloak, and boots. His bulky toga had been left at home, folded in a wardrobe chest. There was no room for it in his saddlebags, and it was better not to draw attention to himself with fine clothes. Two companions rode with Caesar: his valet, Tithonus, and an ex-gladiator named Taurus, on loan from Uncle Cotta's bodyguards.

They were headed for the Sabine hill country, where Aurelia's family had come from. While Caesar hastily changed his clothes for the journey, Aurelia drew up a list of people who might hide him. As the slaves waited in the alley with the horses, Aurelia had handed Caesar a small but heavy pouch. "For bribes," she said. "And if you run out of money, promise them as much as you need to."

Five miles north of the city walls, Caesar's horse's hooves clattered on a bridge over the Tiber River. He'd traveled outside Rome many times in his eighteen years, but usually in the other direction—to the Caesar estates in the Campagnia region, and to Uncle Marius's seaside villa. The Flaminian Way crossed the Tiber River again farther north, Caesar knew. But they wouldn't stay on the highway that long. Too easy for Sulla's bounty hunters to follow swiftly and track him down.

The February day was cold and gray, but at least no farmers were out in the fields to inform a bounty hunter that a young man had passed by, traveling fast. As Gaius Caesar rode through the bleak winter landscape, he watched impatiently for each milestone to appear. He glimpsed inscriptions on the milestones, letting travelers know who deserved the credit for improving this road. Aediles were the Roman officials in charge of keeping up the highways, and the position of aedile was a good way for a young politician to get his name known. Would G. Julius Caesar ever have the chance of running for aedile, let alone of having his name on a milestone?

Never mind. The first order of business was staying alive. "It's starting to rain, Master," Tithonus pointed out. Caesar was afraid they were still too close to Rome to stop. But before they were soaked through, he turned off the road and found a dry spot in a deserted hut.

Day after day, month after month, Gaius Caesar and his companions lived on the run. He wondered at first if anyone would risk taking in a fugitive, but his mother had chosen carefully. Only one person on Aurelia's list refused to give him shelter.

The first host hid them in an unused stable.

Another had his steward give them blankets and show them to a cave in the woods at the edge of his estate. Still another allowed Caesar a cubicle in the main house, but he made Caesar pretend to be a hired tutor from Alexandria. At least it was somewhat amusing to talk in an Egyptian accent and expound at tedious length about classical Greek diction.

Caesar never stayed more than a few days in any one place, whether he got warning of bounty hunters looking for him or not. As Taurus, his bodyguard, put it, "They're counting on you to settle somewhere, to get comfortable and unwary. Then they'll pounce."

One host handed Caesar a letter from his mother, sent to the host weeks ago and kept in case Caesar showed up.

My dearest son, I pray to your protector Venus that you are well and safe. Don't lose heart; our influential friends are working to change a certain person's mind and bring you back to us. If this letter reaches you, don't try to reply.

Cold February gave way to rainy March. Suddenly the rolling hills were green instead of brown, and cowbells clanged as Caesar rode by pastures. Gazing at the scenery, Gaius Caesar thought about the problem of land reform. Land reform bills were almost impossible to get through the Senate, because the wealthy plantation owners—many of them senators—didn't want public lands to be given to veterans. They wanted to buy the land cheaply to swell their own holdings. But veterans without land, and small farmers pushed off their farms, turned into unemployed mobs in Rome. *Rome will never have peace,* Caesar thought, *without land reform.*

April was unusually warm that year, and soon clouds of mosquitoes hovered over the meadows and whined under the trees. Caesar and his bodyguard and valet, always on the move and often sleeping outdoors, got used to swatting and scratching. By May, Caesar was burning with fever, then shivering with chills.

"It's the four-day fever," said Taurus. "We get that a lot around Capua."

Fortunately, by that time, Gaius Caesar wasn't far from the villa of Aurelia's older cousin. Cousin Aurelia, a widow, managed her own estate. "You are welcome here, young Gaius," she said. "Sulla's thugs don't scare *me*." While his valet tucked blankets around him, she brewed for Caesar with her own hands an herbal tea of feverfew.

Two days later, as Caesar was still shivering and burning in bed, a band of Sulla's men rode up to the front door. Caesar, warned by Taurus, dragged himself out of bed. Cousin Aurelia rushed in. "Come, Gaius! You must hide in the well."

But Caesar waved her off. "No, Cousin. I'll talk to them. Don't worry." To his bodyguard he said, "Let me lean on your arm. It'll be harder for them to cut off my head if I'm standing up." He met the bounty hunters in the courtyard. "Welcome to my family's home, citizens,"

Caesar told the thuggish-looking men.

One man put his hand on his sword hilt when he saw Gaius Caesar, but the leader motioned him to wait. Caesar went on: "I think I can make your trip from Rome worthwhile."

As Caesar had hoped, the bounty hunters were reasonable men. They'd come here to cut off his head, carry it to Rome, and trade it in for the bounty. But for a bribe amounting to 10 percent more than the bounty, they'd be just as happy to let him keep his head. They swore to it, on the graves of their ancestors.

After the price had been settled and Tithonus had fetched a bag of silver coins, Caesar urged the intruders to stay for a cup of wine. Even though he was weak and dizzy, Caesar was eager to hear fresh news from Rome. It seemed that Marcus Cicero, now a young lawyer, was making a name for himself in court. In Africa, the young general Pompey (the same brave man who'd divorced his wife at a word from Sulla, Caesar thought) had won brilliant victories for Rome. Now he was demanding that the Senate award him a triumph, a victory parade.

As the soldiers' hoofbeats faded away down the hill, Caesar ordered his valet to pack. Cousin Aurelia begged him to go back to bed at least overnight, but Taurus agreed with his master. "I wouldn't trust those scum from here to the pigpen. Likely as not, they'll tell another band where you are and let them collect your head and the bounty."

Caesar smiled weakly. "Right—that wouldn't bother the graves of their ancestors."

"Especially since their ancestors were sewer rats," put in Tithonus. "And of course they'd expect a cut of the bounty."

So Gaius Caesar kept moving. The countryside blossomed; bees hummed and crops ripened in the orchards and fields. Caesar was so thin and weak now that Taurus had to boost him into the saddle, and his mind floated along instead of leaping from thought to thought.

One hot June day Caesar lay on a mossy

stream bank near the country house of a friend of Uncle Cotta's second cousin by marriage. Caesar was no longer suffering from fevers and chills, but the disease had sapped his energy. Taurus kept watch from the crotch of a nearby willow tree.

Hearing the rustle of long grass at the top of the slope, Caesar opened his eyes to see a man in traveling boots striding toward him. Was the man a messenger, warning Caesar to move to yet another hideout before the next bounty hunter arrived? Or was he a bounty hunter, come to cut off his head and deliver it to Sulla? Either way, Caesar decided, he would not move.

Taurus jumped down from the willow and put his hand on his sword hilt. Seeing this, the stranger stopped out of reach. "Gaius Caesar?" he called. "A letter from the Lady Aurelia, sir."

A letter from Mother? Caesar sat up. Taurus, still suspicious, received the letter case from the messenger, broke the seal, and checked inside.

"I've heard of them booby-trapping letters with poison-tipped needles." He handed the roll of papyrus to Caesar.

It was no trick; the letter was written in Aurelia's script. Her handwriting was unusually sloppy, though, as if she couldn't wait to send the letter on its way. Ever since Caesar had fled Rome, she'd been tirelessly nagging every relative and friend who might have influence with Sulla. Now, she reported, the combined pleading of Uncle Cotta, the Head Vestal, and many others had finally taken effect.

"All right, all right!" Sulla had finally told Uncle Cotta. "Have it your way. Gaius Julius Caesar is now pardoned. Only remember: This man you're so eager to save will be the downfall of the aristocracy—of the system you and I have worked to uphold. In this Caesar, there is more than one Marius."

"My dear son," Aurelia wrote, "if you have even one Marius inside, you must be very uncomfortable!"

Caesar laughed. He felt better already. "Taurus! Tell Tithonus to pack. We're going home."

As it turned out, Gaius Caesar stayed in Rome only long enough to regain his strength. The following March he set off for the port of Brundisium. Caesar had been sorry to leave home again so soon, but his mother and Cornelia both begged him to go. It had become clear that as long as Sulla was dictator, Gaius Caesar would always be under suspicion. Caesar would be much safer far away from Rome.

So Aurelia had urged Uncle Cotta to have a talk with his associate Marcus Minucius Thermus, who owed him a favor or two. Marcus Thermus was the new governor of Asia Minor, appointed by the Senate to get the province back in order. Cotta did have a talk with him, and Governor Thermus did ask Caesar to join his staff as a junior officer.

Early one morning a fleet of Roman galleys

cast off from the quay in Brundisium. Orders rang out, the rigging creaked, and sails snapped in an offshore wind. Gaius Caesar stood on the deck of the commander's ship, filling his lungs with the salt-tanged air. As the fog lifted he gazed back at the ships following, their rows of oars dipping in unison and the sails unfolding. The walled city of Brundisium seemed to shrink behind them.

Another junior officer joined Caesar at the ship's railing. "To Neptune, for a fair voyage." He poured a splash of wine into the waves, then offered the wineskin to Caesar.

Caesar smiled and shook his head. "And thanks be to Jupiter for sending us to Asia Minor, hm? We'll have it all: military experience, provincial government—"

"And Ephesus!" interrupted an older officer on Caesar's other side. Caesar recognized him as one of the governor's deputies. "Wait till you boys see the great temple of Artemis at Ephesus. Why, it must be ten times the size of our Temple of Jupiter on Capitoline Hill, and all of the finest marble. Towering columns running all the way around the building."

"It may be a fine temple," said the young officer, "but the Ephesians don't honor Artemis, protector of their city, the way they should. Some Romans fled into the temple for sanctuary, during the war with Mithridates, and the Ephesians killed them right on the altar."

Caesar had heard about the temple, although not from his father. His father hadn't talked much about Ephesus. But then, Gaius Caesar the Elder had never talked much about anything. Other travelers, such as Gnipho, had told Caesar about the glories of Ephesus.

"And on the way, we'll stop at Athens," continued the experienced officer. "Too bad Sulla's army sacked the city so thoroughly, although it was the Athenians' own fault, for siding with Mithridates. In years past, you could pick up some real art treasures in Athens."

Now that they were under way, Gaius Caesar was excited. He'd never been outside

Italy before, and he was headed for Asia Minor. The ship slid out of the harbor and into the Adriatic Sea, which glittered in the rising sun. The world was opening up for Gaius Julius Caesar.

CHAPTER 10
THE CITIZEN'S CROWN

80–77 B.C.

"Why can't Rome have a permanent theater like this?" Caesar asked a friend. "Why should Romans have to watch plays in flimsy wooden theaters?" They were waiting for the performance in seats reserved for Governor Thermus's staff, close to the three-story stage of Ephesus's public theater. Built with stone into the slope of the hills behind the city, it could seat many thousands of people. The acoustics were so good that even the commoners in the worst seats could hear every word from the stage.

"Oh, you know what the crusty old men in Rome say," answered the other junior officer. "They think that permanent theaters would corrupt our Republican moral fiber. Probably Cato the Censor's idea."

In between his duties, Caesar had had some time to explore the city of Ephesus. He kept comparing Ephesus in his mind with Rome, which was a much larger city but not as pleasant to live in. But Rome could be a splendid city, he thought, if the right people were in charge.

It seemed to Caesar that the Ephesians had enough moral fiber, or at least as much as the Romans. He was getting to know the Ephesians, since one of his duties was to decide which petitioners should be allowed an appointment with Governor Thermus. Caesar was pleased that some of the local people remembered Gaius Julius Caesar the Elder as a decent governor.

Before long, Caesar had a new assignment: He was to travel to Bithynia, a kingdom between Asia Minor and Pontus, to collect a fleet of ships from King Nicomedes. Governor Thermus wanted the fleet for his campaign against Mytilene. Although Sulla had defeated

Mithridates and forced him to give up Asia Minor, there were still pockets of resistance to Roman rule. Governor Thermus was especially eager to take back the island of Lesbos and its city, Mytilene.

On his way north to the Black Sea, Caesar traveled through Pergamum, a city whose library was even finer than the library at Ephesus. Caesar wrote Uncle Cotta from that city, "Why shouldn't Rome have a library like this?" Rome had no public library at all.

Troy was also on his way north, so Gaius Caesar got his boyhood wish to visit the fabled city of the *Iliad.* There was nothing there now to remind a traveler of Homer's epic, "but I made a sacrifice there, anyway, in honor of our ancestor Aeneas," Caesar wrote his mother.

When Caesar arrived at Nicomedes's palace in Bithynia, the king received him at once. "Of course I remember you, my dear Gaius Caesar! We met at that magnificent reception at your uncle Sextus's, after my appearance before the Senate."

Governor Thermus had ordered Caesar to receive the fleet from Nicomedes and escort it back to Ephesus, and at first that was what Caesar intended to do. But before he knew it, Caesar fell into the way of life at Nicomedes's court. Caesar had thought his friends in Rome enjoyed luxury, with their soft cushions, and rooms lighted with scented oil. But Nicomedes had a larger idea of luxury. He bought music by the most gifted cithara and flute players, conversation with the most brilliant natural philosophers, entertainment by the most talented dramatists.

"Isn't this what life is for?" Nicomedes said when Caesar commented. "To enjoy the best of everything?"

"Not according to Cato the Censor." Caesar laughed. "In Rome, life is for getting up at dawn, practicing swordplay on the Field of Mars, attending a Senate meeting for a good, long squabble, eating a wholesome dinner of porridge, and going to bed early."

Time passed. A messenger brought a letter from Governor Thermus, wanting to know when he could expect Caesar back with the promised fleet. Caesar sent back a vague excuse, assuring the governor that he'd return soon, very soon.

Late one morning, when Caesar was touring the palace gardens with a renowned sculptor, a messenger appeared. "Letters from Ephesus?" asked Caesar. He was afraid that the governor was going to order him to return immediately, no more nonsense.

But, instead, these were letters from Rome. One each from Aurelia and Cornelia, rolled up in the same canister; one from Uncle Cotta; and one from a school friend. They all mentioned the latest triumphal parade. Pompey had celebrated it for his victories in Africa.

Pompey had a nerve, the letters said, demanding a triumph when he hadn't even reached the rank of praetor. "Do you know what he's calling himself?" wrote Aurelia. "Pompeius Magnus—Pompey the Great!"

In Uncle Cotta's opinion, Pompey had made a fool of himself over the triumph. He tried to put on an especially splendid show by hitching his gilded chariot to elephants on the Field of Mars, where the parade began. As it turned out, the elephants couldn't squeeze through the Fontinal Gate. The crowd watched and laughed while the elephants were unhitched and replaced with the usual white horses.

But Gaius Caesar, reading the letters, didn't laugh. Pompey, only six years older than Caesar, had won great glory for himself. Caesar was wasting time. "Start packing," Caesar told his valet. "We're going to Mytilene."

Caesar arrived in time to report to Lucullus, the Roman commander, before the siege of Mytilene began. The allure of Nicomedes's court forgotten, Caesar focused all his attention on the battle. As he watched General Lucullus give orders, Caesar could see that the man understood military strategy. And Lucullus was

159

decisive and forceful; the officers under him knew exactly what their orders were.

But in Caesar's opinion, Lucullus missed many chances to make his men devoted to him. He didn't share his soldiers' hardships. In the past, he hadn't allowed them to feast and plunder after a victory. He never strolled among the tents to chat with the troops.

No, General Lucullus's troops didn't love him, but the Romans won the siege of Mytilene anyway. *"Overwhelming force, my boy,"* Caesar seemed to hear Old Marius saying. That was why Governor Thermus had demanded the extra fleet from Nicomedes.

During his first real battle, Caesar found himself thrilled and calm at the same time. It was almost like a good game of trigon, with balls coming at him from different directions, and all his senses sharpened. And the danger only made the game all the more exciting.

Leading an assault on the walls of the city, Caesar saw one of his centurions wounded.

The man fell to the ground with an arrow in his leg, and an enemy soldier loomed over him with a spear. Caesar cut the attacker down with his sword, boosted the wounded soldier onto his horse, and galloped behind the lines to safety. At the time, in the excitement of the battle, Caesar hardly thought about what he'd done. Dropping the centurion off at the hospital tent, he wheeled his horse and dashed back into the smoke and dust with his sword drawn.

After the battle, Governor Thermus arrived on Lesbos to congratulate Lucullus and his troops. Thermus gave a speech to the gathered army, and he awarded honors to Romans who'd showed great valor. Caesar stood at attention before the governor, but at the same time gazing toward the mainland and Mount Ida. Ida was supposed to be the peak from which Jupiter (or Zeus, as the Greeks called him) had watched the Trojan War.

Then Caesar heard his name. "To Gaius Julius Caesar—the Citizen's Crown, for saving the life of a fellow Roman at great risk to himself." As Thermus set a crown of oak leaves on Caesar's head, the ranks of soldiers shouted their approval.

On the trip back to Ephesus, Caesar heard fresh news from Rome. "Can you believe it?" a fellow officer asked Caesar. "Sulla announced his retirement."

"A dictator can't retire!" exclaimed Caesar. "He slaughters half the citizens of the Republic, seizes complete control of the Roman state— and now he thinks he can retire to his seaside villa in Puteoli?" But all the reports from Rome confirmed that Sulla was doing exactly that.

Whatever Sulla was doing, Caesar was determined to pursue his own career. He felt he needed more military experience, and the battles in Asia Minor seemed to be over for the moment, so he requested a transfer. He transferred to Cilicia, a string of military outposts on the southeast coast of Anatolia. Their main function was to fend off the pirates and keep the trade routes open for Rome. Caesar would serve on the staff of Governor Servilius Isauricus.

The voyage from Ephesus to Governor Servilius's headquarters in Tarsus took longer than Caesar expected. The ship crept along the south coast like a timid crab, darting into this cove or behind that point at the least hint of trouble. Caesar complained to the captain. "You're sailing a Roman warship, not a pleasure yacht."

"With all due respect, sir," said the captain, "you haven't seen the pirates' ships. This coast is their territory. They're built for speed, they can put on twice the sail that I can, and they're packed with desperate cutthroats. If you want to arrive at Tarsus at all, slow and cautious is the way to do it."

Romans going slowly and cautiously, in fear of pirates? *This is intolerable,* Caesar thought. *This must change.*

At the first staff dinner in Tarsus, Caesar met another junior officer named Lucius

Sergius Catalina. Lucius Catalina, like Gaius Caesar, was from a patrician family. But they had even less money than the Caesars, as Caesar remembered.

"Please satisfy my curiosity," Catalina said with a teasing grin. "Why, in the name of Diana of Ephesus, would you ask to be transferred from such a fascinating city to a provincial outpost like Tarsus?"

Caesar laughed, but he explained: "I loved Ephesus, but there's more to life than beautiful temples and exciting drama. I need more military experience. Right now, the greatest threat to Rome is the pirates—don't you think?"

"I suppose you're right," said Catalina. Then he muttered, so low that Caesar hardly heard him, "Unless it's the greed of the upper classes. We make enemies for Rome."

Caesar had to admit that Catalina had a point. He'd come to Asia Minor with the same question as many Romans: Why do they hate us so much? Why had the provincials slaughtered eighty thousand Roman citizens and welcomed Mithridates with open arms?

During Caesar's months in Asia Minor, the answer had become plain: Romans had governed the province badly. Maybe Caesar's own father hadn't been so bad, but most governors taxed the local people into poverty. These Roman governors laid on such a heavy tax burden that even rich, thriving cities were forced to mortgage their public theaters. The Romans drained the profits from the local ranches, industries, fisheries—and poured the money directly into their own coffers.

As it turned out, Gaius Caesar spent only a few months in Cilicia. A military courier brought big news from Rome: Sulla the Lucky was dead. To Caesar's surprise, Sulla had *not* been slain by a vengeful relative of Cousin Marius or some other victim. He hadn't been slain at all. Sulla had been lucky to the last, dying peacefully in his bed at Puteoli, after enjoying a gourmet banquet with his favorite actresses and poets.

The news changed Caesar's plans: He could now safely return to Rome to pursue his political career. A letter from Marcus Aemilius Lepidus, a consul this year, invited Caesar to join him in overturning the conservative laws Sulla had passed. Caesar was all for overturning Sulla's work, but he wasn't sure he should ally himself with Lepidus. He needed to get back to Rome and talk the situation over with his mother and uncles.

Now that Caesar was finally returning to his family, he could hardly wait. He could almost smell the hyacinth scent in Cornelia's hair. He wanted to mount a winged horse like Pegasus and leap over the Aegean Sea, over Greece, over the Adriatic Sea, all the way to Rome.

The day before Caesar's departure, Catalina came to his quarters. "Did you hear about Sulla's funeral?" asked a sardonic voice. Caesar glanced up to see Catalina leaning against the door frame with folded arms. "Pompey brought his body to Rome on a gold-decorated litter."

"Yes," said Caesar. "They say that Sulla was

cremated as a Roman hero on the Field of Mars, although Consul Lepidus tried his best to prevent it. Not only that—my mother writes that the women of Rome, by decree of the Senate, have to wear black for a year as a sign of mourning." He could imagine how bitter that was for Aunt Julia and for Licinia, Cousin Marius's widow.

"The gods are laughing at us," said Catalina. "That butcher's head should be on a pike in the Forum."

Caesar looked at Catalina with a thoughtful smile. There was something over-reckless about this man. It was one thing to be daring, but Catalina seemed to risk danger just for the sake of the risk, like a gambler bent on losing all his money. "Maybe so," said Caesar. "But look on the bright side: Sulla *is* dead. Now I can go home."

CHAPTER 11
PRISONER OF PIRATES

77–71 B.C.

Back in Rome, Caesar was glad he'd decided to steer clear of Lepidus and his ambitious plans. Caesar agreed with Lepidus's politics: giving back power to the tribunes of the people, handing out grain to the poor people of Rome, and restoring the rights of Sulla's victims. But Lepidus made the mistake of thinking he could lead a popular rebellion in Italy and take over Rome. In the end, his army was defeated just outside the city.

Incompetent, thought Caesar. *If I were going to march on Rome, I'd do it quickly, with overwhelming force.*

Meanwhile, Cornelia gave birth to their

first child, a daughter. Girls were always given the clan name, so she was named Julia, like Caesar's aunt and sisters.

"I'm not going to hand her over to a nursemaid," said Cornelia, holding out the little bundle for Caesar to see. "I'm going to take care of her myself, just the way your mother did with you."

"My mother's a wise woman," said Caesar, putting a finger out for the baby to grab. He wanted a male heir, of course, but there was plenty of time. He himself was Aurelia's third child.

Now that the turmoil of Lepidus's rebellion was ended, Gaius Caesar launched his political career. The first step was to present a case in court as an advocate, a lawyer. For his opening case, Caesar charged a former governor of Macedonia, Gnaeus Cornelius Dolabella, with corruption.

Caesar's advisers were dismayed. "You can't possibly win," said Aurelia. "Your uncle Cotta has agreed to defend Dolabella. Besides, Dolabella can afford to buy and sell the praetor and the jury ten times over."

Caesar said calmly, "I don't expect to win, Mother. I expect to make life difficult for Dolabella, that bottom-feeding, lick-spittle tool of Sulla's. And I expect to make a name for myself."

One thing Caesar had learned, during his time abroad, was that most Roman governors ran their provinces with corruption and greed. Still, in public speeches, Roman officials always preached of spreading the blessings of Roman justice throughout the world. So Caesar attacked Dolabella as if he expected Romans to recoil in shock and horror at the proof of his corruption.

As everyone predicted, Dolabella was acquitted. Even though Caesar had expected it, he felt let down when the verdict was announced. As he walked out of the Forum that afternoon, he wondered what he'd actually accomplished.

But as Caesar was about to step into his litter, a familiar voice called out, "Gaius Caesar!" It was Marcus Cicero, back from Rhodes just in time to hear Caesar's first speech. "Congratulations!" said Cicero. "You really gave it to that corrupt old scoundrel. It makes me sick the way our governors fleece the provinces."

Caesar smiled ruefully. "But the corrupt old scoundrel won."

"Well, you knew that would happen," said Cicero. "Of course he bought his acquittal. But you still performed admirably."

Caesar bowed. "I only hope someday I'll be as effective an advocate as you were in defending Sextus Roscius. The fame of your victory reached us way off in Asia Minor. Now, *that* was brilliant—and fairly courageous, attacking a man under Sulla's protection while Sulla was still dictator."

They stood talking beside the litter for some time. Cicero urged Caesar to publish his speech against Dolabella, and also to think about studying with Apollonius of Rhodes.

Gaius Caesar prosecuted another case of corruption against another of Sulla's henchmen, and then it seemed wise for him to leave Rome again. "You made a name for yourself, all right," said Uncle Cotta dryly. He was running for consul this year. "If you'd won the case against Dolabella, you'd be a dead man. As it is, he's determined to bring charges against you."

So once again, Gaius Caesar said good-bye to his family and set off on the long journey to Asia Minor. This time he didn't remain in Ephesus, but took passage on a merchant ship bound for the island of Rhodes. As Cicero advised, he intended to study rhetoric with Apollonius Molon.

The day after the merchant ship left the city of Miletus, a sailor at the prow shouted and pointed. Darting from a cove on a nearby island, a large, sleek ship was bearing down on them. Bright metal flashed from the strange ship's masts and oars, and it flew a purple flag.

"Pirates!" exclaimed the captain. "Neptune sink them all!" But Caesar thought he didn't seem especially surprised, or even alarmed. The pirates hopped aboard, waving their swords rather casually. Without being told, the crew began to carry the cargo up from the hold.

The pirate chief pointed at Caesar. "You rich Roman, you're coming with us. Tell your men to inform your friends that your ransom is twenty talents. Not a sestertius less."

Twenty talents was ten times as much as the price on Caesar's head when he was fleeing from Sulla's bounty hunters. A wicked idea leaped into Caesar's mind, and he looked down his nose at the pirate. "*Twenty* talents? Do you know whom you're talking to? I am Gaius Julius Caesar. You'd be a fool to hand me over for less than fifty talents."

The blank look on the pirate chief's face was priceless. As he hesitated, the other pirates glanced at one another. What kind of a man was this who demanded to be ransomed for more than twice as much? Caesar smiled inwardly. This was like swordplay, with old Postumus Rufus calling, "Keep him off balance!"

"Have it your way—fifty talents." The pirate chief decided to treat Caesar as a harmless fool. "You drive a hard bargain." He guffawed at his own wit, and his crew joined in.

So the merchant ship, with Caesar's retainers, turned back toward Miletus to raise the enormous ransom. Caesar settled in at the pirates' camp, on an inlet hidden by the craggy coastline.

The pirates had captured and demanded ransom from many wealthy Romans, but they'd never met one like Caesar. He acted more like a guest at a seaside resort than a prisoner of pirates. He had Tithonus shave him every day and keep his clothes clean and neat. He composed long poems in classical Greek and recited them to the pirates. If the pirates caroused when he was sleeping, Caesar ordered them to be quiet.

The moon waxed and waned in a full cycle. One evening the pirate chief invited Caesar to share a pitcher of wine in front of his tent. The pirate proposed the first toast. "Here's to Mithridates the Liberator—may he rise again!" He poured out a libation on the sand, then drained his cup.

Caesar's eyes narrowed. He knew very well that the pirates' federation was friendly with Mithridates of Pontus. But it was too much to hear him hailed as a hero. "Here's to my protector Venus Fortuna, who fogged these pirates' minds and caused their folly!" He, too, poured a libation before sipping his wine.

"What d'you mean, 'folly'?" growled the pirate. "You're my prisoner, Roman, don't forget."

"Exactly." Gaius Caesar took a sip of wine. "Mmm, excellent vintage. This must be the wine you stole from my stores." Before the pirate chief could shout at him, he went on smoothly, "By 'folly,' I mean that you should have killed me instead of holding me for ransom. After I'm ransomed, I'll raise enough troops to outnumber you two to one and come back to capture you." He smiled pleasantly around the campfire, where the other pirates sat on the sand. "And then I'll execute every one of you for the capital crime of piracy."

The pirate chief stared at him. Then he burst out laughing. "What a joker you are, Caesar! You had me fooled there for a moment. As if you could even find this camp again!"

The pirate's men roared with laughter too. "Haw, haw! He'll execute us!"

As the moon began to grow again, Caesar's men returned with the ransom. The pirates took their fifty talents and let him go. Caesar sailed straight for the mainland, gathered a large force of soldiers, and guided them to the cove where the pirates' camp was hidden. The surprised pirates were easily taken prisoner.

Caesar didn't have any authority to execute criminals in the name of Rome, and he wanted to follow the proper procedure. So he sent a report to the current governor of Asia Minor, requesting permission to execute the pirates. When his report was ignored, Caesar realized that the pirates' federation must have paid off the governor as well as the sea captain.

Now Caesar was more determined than ever, and he went ahead with the executions. However, he didn't want to apply the usual punishment for piracy—crucifixion—which was a cruel, lingering death. Caesar ordered the pirates' throats to be cut first so they wouldn't suffer. "For the sake of their gracious hospitality to me," Caesar explained to the centurion.

At Rhodes, Caesar found a center of culture. With introductions from Apollonius, Caesar met many people who were the best in their field. For instance, a well-known sculptor took Caesar to see the most famous sight on the island. That was the Colossus of Rhodes, a one-hundred-foot bronze statue of the city's patron god, the sun god Helios.

Years ago, an earthquake had knocked the Colossus from its pedestal on a high point above the harbor. Caesar was fascinated to know how the Colossus had been built, and how the Colossus compared with other huge statues, such as ones of the pharaohs in Egypt. Also, could the earthquake damage have been prevented?

As the days went on, constant practice with Apollonius improved Caesar's speaking skills. But he grew restless. A voice in the back of his head whispered, *You are twenty-six. At twenty-six, Alexander the Great had conquered most of the world.*

Of course Alexander had been one of a kind, almost a demigod, and he'd been dead for three hundred years. But there was a man alive today whom Caesar constantly measured himself against: the general who called himself Magnus, "Great." Pompey the Great. Only six years older than Caesar, Pompey had heard his army acclaim him as *imperator*, "victorious general." Pompey had ridden in triumph through the streets of Rome.

At least Caesar had won a kind of fame, he

thought wryly. According to letters from his family and friends, the story of Gaius Caesar and the pirates was all over Rome.

One day, the news in the letters from Rome was sad. Caesar's uncle Cotta, former consul and member of the College of Pontiffs, had died. Gaius Caesar thought of Uncle Cotta and their walks around the city. *Always honor Alexander,* Caesar seemed to hear him say.

On the practical side, Uncle Cotta's death was an opportunity for Gaius Caesar. There was now an opening in the College of Pontiffs, and Caesar hoped to be appointed to fill it. The pontiffs, overseeing the state religion of Rome, wielded quite a bit of political power. Through their interpretations of omens and sacred writings, the priests could decide whether a certain day was lucky or unlucky. Romans took this very seriously, and the Senate would never meet on an "unlucky" day. Neither would an army set out, or would banks open for business.

In the meantime, Rome was in a state of

terror about the slave rebellion in Italy. Spartacus, a slave gladiator training at Capua, had led a successful breakout from the training camp. They were a small band at first, but more and more slaves joined them until the rebels were an army of thousands. Mithridates of Pontus, still interested in making trouble for Rome, was feeling Spartacus out about joining forces.

While Caesar was waiting to hear about the pontiff appointment, Mithridates invaded Bithynia again. At the same time, he sent a military force south into Asia Minor. Caesar, glad for an excuse to do something, dropped his studies. He took a fast ship back to the mainland of Asia Minor and raised troops to fight Mithridates's invaders. No one had given him the authority to do this, but he was confident that the Roman government wouldn't complain if Caesar's little army performed well. In fact, Caesar saved several towns in the southern part of the province.

Then good news came from the honorable

College of Pontiffs: Gaius Julius Caesar was the new appointee. Although it was now midwinter, bad weather for traveling, Caesar set out at once.

Back in Rome, Caesar learned that Pompey was a bigger hero than ever. He'd won important victories against rebels in Spain, and he'd helped Crassus subdue Spartacus's slave rebellion. Pompey was cheered everywhere he went. The Senate voted to allow him another triumphal parade.

Caesar also learned that Marcus Licinius Crassus was furious about Pompey's popularity. Crassus was the general who'd actually quelled Spartacus's slave rebellion, wiping out twelve thousand rebels in the final battle. Caesar thought Crassus might be helpful to him as a political ally since he was the richest man in Rome. Also, Crassus was in a position of power since he and Pompey had been elected consuls for the coming year.

On the day of Pompey's triumph, the last

day of December, Caesar went to the Forum to see the parade. Marcus Crassus, as consul-elect, was watching from a seat of honor in the loggia of one of the state buildings. He noticed Caesar and beckoned him to come up and join him.

Below, spectators dressed all in white crowded the stands and covered the steps of the temples. The monuments and temple porticos were decked with evergreen garlands, and incense rose in the chilly air. A shout rippled through the crowd: "Pompey! Pompey the Great is coming!"

"Pompey the *Great*," snorted Crassus. "It's ridiculous that the Senate even allowed an upstart like him to run for consul. They're afraid, the spineless fools—afraid he'd turn his army on them."

As Crassus spoke, Pompey came into sight at the beginning of the Sacred Way. His profile was noble under the laurel wreath, his face as radiant as his gilded chariot. The crowd roared, "Pom-pey Mag-nus! Pom-pey Mag-nus!"

"I see he decided on horses this time," remarked Caesar.

Crassus's sour expression changed to a snide smile. "Instead of those elephants that got stuck in the Fontinal Gate last time, you mean." He chuckled, then sighed. "Imagine, I'm going to have to serve as coconsul for an entire year with this small-time Alexander the Great."

Caesar agreed that Pompey was full of himself, but he had to admire Pompey's astonishing military feats. However, Caesar wasn't about to defend Pompey to Crassus. If the two consuls didn't get along, they might be more inclined to link up with someone else—possibly Caesar.

For now, Caesar was bound for Spain. He'd been elected as one of the quaestors, or treasury officials, and assigned to work for the governor of Further Spain. A quaestorship was a necessary step up the political ladder, but it wouldn't be a glamorous job. Besides, he'd have to leave Cornelia again, as well as their eight-year-old daughter. More and more Caesar delighted in little Julia, so bright and loving and so much fun.

Before Gaius Caesar could leave for Spain, his aunt Julia, widow of Old Marius, died. Usually the funerals of women were private, but Caesar decided to give his aunt a public ceremony, with a full procession and funeral oration. This was an opportunity to honor Uncle Marius as well as Aunt Julia, and to get attention for himself.

As was customary, the funeral procession through Rome was led by actors, wearing the masks of the revered dead in the family. The watching crowds gasped as they recognized the rumpled features of Old Marius. Sulla the dictator had passed laws, still on the books, forbidding the display of any images of his enemy. The people burst into cheers.

In the funeral oration, Caesar praised Aunt Julia's ancestry—which was also his own. On her mother's side, he said, she was descended from the first Roman kings. On her father's side, she was descended from the hero Aeneas and the goddess Venus. Without exactly saying so, Gaius Julius Caesar made the point that *he* came from a line of kings and gods.

Shortly after Aunt Julia's funeral, Gaius Caesar suffered a deeper loss. His wife, Cornelia, died. Caesar was grief-stricken. The only person who could comfort him was his daughter, Julia.

While public funerals even for older women were unusual, for younger women they were unheard of. Against tradition, Caesar held a public funeral for his wife. Cornelia's father, Cinna, had also been a bitter enemy of Sulla's, but again Caesar boldly displayed his image in the funeral procession. Caesar spoke frankly to the crowds in the Forum about how dear Cornelia had been to him. For her, he had defied the dictator Sulla, lost Cornelia's dowry—and almost lost his life. Caesar's voice shook as he spoke.

Among the people listening to him, there were many eyes shining with tears. They were deeply touched by this young man's affection for his wife. But they also wept because they remembered Sulla's rule of terror. Friends of theirs, too, had appeared on the dreaded "death list." Relatives of theirs had been hunted down and killed for the bounty.

Gaius Caesar was still grieving inside, but he had been trained to overcome his feelings and do his duty. The Roman Republic expected him to serve as quaestor. Because of the two funerals, he was already late in reporting to C. Antistius Vetus, the governor of Further Spain.

"I'll look for your letters, dearest girl," Caesar told his daughter as he kissed her good-bye. "Help your grandmother keep an eye on things while I'm away."

"Be well, Gaius," said his mother. "Send me some embroidered Spanish linen." Aurelia would never shed a tear in public; she was too much of a patrician lady. But Caesar knew she had loved Cornelia almost as much as he had, and that she would miss her son all the more now that her daughter-in-law was gone.

After arriving in Further Spain and reporting to Governor Vetus, Caesar began traveling from town to town. His job was to hold tribunals, judge property disputes, and perform other minor legal functions. Although Caesar grudged being away from Rome that year, he enjoyed Spain more than he'd expected. Unlike the people of Asia Minor, who secretly thought they were superior to their conquerors, Spaniards *loved* Rome. Everywhere he went in Spain, Caesar found Spaniards who wanted to become Roman citizens. They spoke Latin, they gave their children Roman names, and they wore togas with pride.

And why not let them become citizens? thought Caesar. These people would make good, loyal Romans. Take Balbus, a friend Caesar made when he visited the port of Gades. Balbus was as wealthy, as well educated, and as well mannered as most of the Roman senators. Furthermore, his mind wasn't stuck in old ways of thinking.

At the end of his stay in Gades, Caesar

wrote to the governor, requesting permission to return to Rome before his year of service was up. Permission was granted, and Caesar went to the local temple of Venus to give thanks. He followed the custom of sleeping in the temple in hopes of having a dream to foretell his future. The next morning, the priests interpreted his dream to mean that he would conquer the world. Caesar was skeptical, especially because this was what he wished to hear. As a member of the College of Pontiffs in Rome, he knew how skillful priests could be at pleasing worshippers.

On his return journey, Caesar traveled through Cisalpine Gaul, the Roman province between the Alps and the Adriatic Sea. Caesar's tutor Gnipho had come from this region, and his uncle Marius had saved it from the Germanic tribes. Like the Spaniards, Caesar noted, the Cisalpine Gauls had embraced the Roman way of life. Naturally, they resented having to pay taxes and fight in Roman armies without citizenship.

As Caesar traveled through Italy, he received a letter from his mother with the latest news from Rome: The Senate had voted to remove the gilded statue of Sulla on horseback from the Forum. Caesar looked forward to seeing that for himself.

CHAPTER 12
THE THREE-HEADED MONSTER

68–59 B.C.

Back in Rome, Gaius Caesar was moved to see how much his daughter, Julia, had grown to look like her mother. Her keen dark eyes were like her father's, but otherwise she had her mother's delicate features. It gave Caesar a pang to think of Julia marrying and leaving his house.

"Yes, before we know it, it'll be time to think of betrothing Julia," said Aurelia to Caesar. "Not that I want to do without her company." She gave her granddaughter a fond glance.

"There's no getting around it, Papa," said Julia. She kissed him on the top of his forehead, where his hair was already receding.

"Only when the time comes, don't pick some boring old goat for me."

Meanwhile, Caesar needed to find a wife for himself. He didn't expect the new wife to replace Cornelia in his heart. Marriage was normally a business arrangement between families, after all, not a love match. This time, instead of a full-blown traditional wedding, he would just have a simple civil ceremony.

Caesar was looking for a wife of high social status, but also one with a large dowry, to help him run for political office. And of course he hoped his new wife would give him a son and heir. Consulting with his mother, Caesar chose a woman named Pompeia, with close ties to the powerful Pompey the Great. She was the granddaughter of the dictator Sulla, which was a drawback, in a way. On the other hand, it would probably make Sulla's shade grind his teeth in the underworld.

Caesar needed a society hostess as a wife, and Pompeia was delighted to fill that role. They gave lavish parties, inviting everyone who could help Caesar win an election. He bought an expensive chef for his kitchen, and he hired the best actors, dancers, and musicians to entertain at his banquets.

As Caesar planned, he was elected curator of the Appian Way. With loans from Marcus Crassus, Caesar poured money into improving this major road. He put up signs on the milestones, pointing out his improvements and gaining the gratitude of all the towns along the road.

Meanwhile, a debate ran on in the Senate: What to do about the pirate problem? Pirates still roamed the Mediterranean Sea at will, seizing Roman merchant ships and holding Roman citizens for ransom. Once they had even dared to raid Ostia, the port of Rome itself. The pirates were allied with Mithridates of Pontus, who, after all these years, was still challenging Roman power in Asia Minor.

A tribune proposed to the Senate that Pompey should lead a large, well-funded army against the pirates. The conservative senators were horrified—they thought Pompey was already too powerful. After he conquered the pirates, what was to keep him from turning his army against Rome, the way Sulla had done? Only Caesar spoke up in the Senate for Pompey.

In the end, the People's Assembly voted to give Pompey the command against the pirates. Caesar was satisfied on two counts: Pompey would now take care of the pirates, and he would remember Caesar as a friend. The next year, the Senate debated whether to give Pompey another major command, this time against Mithridates. Caesar voted for Pompey again, and Marcus Cicero gave one of his eloquent speeches in favor of Pompey.

While Pompey was fighting Rome's battles in the Eastern Mediterranean, Caesar ran for the office of aedile. This position offered an even better chance to gain popularity, because the aediles were in charge of public entertainments in Rome. Caesar needed more money for this campaign, and again Crassus backed him.

As aedile, Caesar put on some of the showiest games that Rome had ever seen. One display consisted of 320 pairs of gladiators, all outfitted in dazzling silver armor. He also took advantage of his office to have Old Marius's war trophies mounted in golden settings and put up in the Forum. The conservative senators were outraged, but the people who had believed in Marius's reforms were delighted.

In spite of all the energy he poured into his political career, Gaius Caesar made a point of keeping up his personal friendships. When a son was born to Marcus Cicero, Caesar wrote a note congratulating him. Caesar himself still had only one child, Julia.

Crassus continued to lend Caesar large sums of money as he began his next political campaign. In the College of Pontiffs, the post of Chief Pontiff was vacant. The problem was, two other members of the College—older, respected nobles—were running for Chief Pontiff. It seemed very doubtful that Caesar could win.

Aurelia usually had great faith in her son, but this time she was worried. "You're already deep in debt. You'll have to borrow so much money for this campaign, how can you ever repay it? We'll be ruined!"

"I suppose I'll just have to win, then," Caesar joked. He launched into the work of campaigning. Caesar had a good idea of how much the other candidates were willing to spend to buy votes, and he spent more. He also made speeches and flooded Rome with flyers and posters, claiming that an ancestor of his had been the original Chief Pontiff of Rome.

One day while walking down the Subura Way with his retinue, Caesar noticed a sign painted on the wall of the carriage-maker's shop: G. JULIUS CAESAR FOR CHIEF PONTIFF. Gratus had died in an outbreak of fever while Caesar was in Spain, but his oldest son, Gratus the Younger, had taken over the business. "I agree with your sentiments, citizen," called Caesar, waving to the carriage-maker. Caesar's scribe made a note to send Gratus a handsome gift.

On election day, Gaius Caesar dressed especially carefully. Tithonus shaved him and arranged his toga in precise folds. The household gathered in the atrium to wish him luck. Seeing the strained expressions on the slaves' faces, Caesar understood that they were afraid for themselves. If he lost the election, they would have to be sold.

Caesar kissed his wife, Pompeia, his daughter, Julia, and finally Aurelia. "Well, Mother, if I don't win this one, don't expect me home for dinner. I'll have to flee the country before my creditors jump me." He glanced at Julia and winked, but she didn't smile. As for Pompeia, she looked as if she regretted having married him.

Aurelia didn't smile either. "May Venus Fortuna be with you, my son."

As it turned out, Caesar won the election by a mile. From now on, he would be in charge of the powerful religious establishment in Rome. He and his household moved into the Chief Pontiff's spacious residence, next to the Regia at one end of the Forum. He would never have to move, because the Chief Pontiff served for life.

The same year that Caesar won election as Chief Pontiff, Cicero was elected consul. By this time, it was clear that Caesar was a leader of the political reformers, while Cicero had allied himself with the conservative senators. Caesar was sorry they were in opposing political factions. As the most talented orator in Rome and a canny politician, Cicero could have been very helpful in Caesar's career. Besides—Caesar had always liked Cicero.

Caesar also thought he could have given Cicero some good advice, if they'd been allies. During his consulship, Cicero attacked a senator named Catalina, the same Lucius Catalina whom Caesar had met in Cilicia. Cicero accused Catalina of the most serious crime: conspiring to overthrow the Republic. With his powerful oratory, Cicero managed to turn the Senate against Catalina. Only Caesar spoke up against condemning Catalina to death. As for Catalina, he fled Rome, while Cicero executed his supporters without a trial.

Caesar thought Cicero had acted unjustly, but he also thought Cicero had made a big political mistake. Although the office of consul was powerful, consuls served for only one year. Caesar knew that Cicero's enemies were already plotting revenge.

That September, Caesar's niece Atia, his sister Julia Minor's daughter, gave birth to a son. Looking at the baby boy, Gaius Octavius, Caesar felt envious. It was beginning to seem that everyone except him could have a son. For instance, his friend Servilia, who happened to be the half sister of his bitter political enemy Cato, had a fine son, Marcus Brutus. A serious boy, Brutus was almost a man now.

The following year Caesar was elected praetor, as his father had been when he was a boy. At the end of that year, Caesar's wife, Pompeia, was involved in a major scandal. During the secret rites of the Good Goddess, for women only, she allowed a man to sneak into the house. Caesar was already disappointed in Pompeia, who had not borne him any children, and now she was an embarrassment to him as Chief Pontiff. He divorced her.

The year after Caesar's praetorship, he served as governor of Further Spain, where bandits were harassing the Roman rulers. In the course of his campaign against the bandits, Caesar sailed his troops from Gades in southern Spain all the way up the coast to attack Brigantium in the north. This was the first time that Roman soldiers had ventured into the Atlantic Ocean.

The rebellion in Spain was only a small rebellion, and Caesar's army was only a small force. Still, Caesar was gratified to discover how well he could command an army. Planning military strategy came naturally to him; he also had a talent for bringing out the best in his staff officers and for inspiring his common soldiers to fight their hardest. When they successfully put down the bandits in Further Spain, Caesar's troops acclaimed him as *imperator,* a general deserving a triumph.

On his return from Further Spain, Caesar would have relished a triumphal parade through the streets of Rome. Pompey had just celebrated his *third* triumph, even more splendid than his first two, for his final defeat of Mithridates and for other victories in the East. The crowds had cheered themselves hoarse as an enormous picture of Pompey, made out of pearls, was paraded past. And the people had gone wild at the sight of Pompey in a purple toga sprinkled with gold stars, wearing a cloak said to belong to Alexander the Great.

But Caesar, because of conflicting laws, couldn't both hold a triumph and register as a candidate for consul. So he gave up his triumph in order to run for consul. With the support of Crassus and Pompey, Caesar won. Finally, he had climbed to the top of the political ladder. Now people would say, "In the year that Gaius Caesar was consul . . ."

Caesar wanted to use his office to reform the Roman political system, which badly needed it. But it seemed hopeless to expect the Senate to enact reforms, because the Senate had such a hard time deciding anything. The only way to reform the Roman Republic, Caesar concluded, was for a few powerful men to take charge. He had the men in mind: Pompey, Crassus, Cicero, and himself.

In the months before he took office as consul, Caesar began to put together a four-way deal. First he approached Pompey. Pompey wanted his veterans rewarded with land, and he wanted Rome to accept the decisions Pompey had made in Asia Minor. Caesar agreed that these actions would be good for the empire as well as Pompey.

Crassus was a little more difficult to draw in, since he hated Pompey so much. Crassus always felt he should have gotten more credit for crushing Spartacus's slave rebellion. However, Crassus was also disgusted with the Senate, and he wanted to help the tax farmers in Asia Minor renegotiate their contracts with Rome. He agreed to join Caesar's group.

Cicero, however, turned down Caesar's proposal. Cicero could not imagine a better government for Rome than the Senate. He believed so fervently in the Roman Republic and its constitution that he would not conspire against them.

Caesar was very sorry that he couldn't persuade Cicero, but he went ahead with a three-way deal. Perhaps, he thought, it was meant to be only three, like the ball game of trigon. As consul, Caesar would support Pompey's and Crassus's goals. In turn, he expected them to support his demands. What he would need the most was protection *after* his year as consul, when his enemies would attack him. If he was a governor, he couldn't be prosecuted, so Caesar wanted the governorship of a major province for several years.

Caesar's first move as consul was to introduce a land-reform bill, giving public lands to Pompey's veterans. To further deepen his ties with the great general, he also married his daughter, Julia, to Pompey. Caesar was glad to see that Pompey genuinely loved his daughter. Julia became very fond of Pompey, too, even though he was much older. "He's so sweet, Papa," she told her father. "So modest and tactful." This was a different side of Pompey than the vain, ruthless man that Caesar knew, but he was happy for Julia.

Caesar's coconsul, a conservative named Bibulus, tried to block all his reforms. But Bibulus was no match for Caesar, who simply carried on all the business of state without him. It was a joke in Rome, that year, that the two consuls were "Julius Caesar" and "Gaius Caesar." Other jokes were made about the triumvirate, or three-man rule, of Pompey, Crassus, and Caesar. One Roman wit called them "the Beast with Three Heads."

That fall, one of the consuls elected for the following year was Lucius Calpurnius Piso. He was a supporter of the triumvirate, and Caesar had just married his daughter, Calpurnia. Caesar knew he would need all the help he could get; his enemies were waiting to cancel all his reforms and bring him down the moment he left office.

With the support of his son-in-law, Pompey, and his father-in-law, Consul Piso, Caesar was awarded the governorship of Cisalpine Gaul and Transalpine Gaul for the next five years. As a governor, Caesar would be immune from legal prosecution. And he would also have opportunities to reap great wealth and military glory.

CHAPTER 13

THE CONQUEST OF GAUL

58–52 B.C.

The Roman Senate never gave Gaius Julius Caesar the authority to conquer Gaul. They only appointed him governor of three provinces: Cisalpine Gaul, the territory now known as northern Italy; Transalpine Gaul, now part of southern France; and Illyricum, along the east coast of the Adriatic Sea. To defend these territories, they assigned to him four legions, or twenty-four thousand soldiers. The rest of Gaul, inhabited by various independent Celtic tribes, stretched from the Spanish border up to the English Channel, and from the Atlantic Ocean to the Rhine River.

On the eastern side of the Rhine lived the warlike German tribes. Caesar's uncle Marius had saved Rome from two of these tribes, the Cimbri and the Teutoni, before Caesar was born. Now the German tribes were pushing westward again. Caesar believed that if Rome didn't conquer Gaul, the Germans would. And if the Germans did take Gaul, they would threaten Rome again.

At this time the Germans were harrying the Helvetii, a Celtic tribe in Eastern Gaul. The Helvetii wanted to migrate across Gaul to a new homeland on the Atlantic coast. But the Gauls in the path of the Helvetian migration were nervous, and they appealed to Rome to protect them. Furthermore, the Romans wanted the Helvetii to stay in place as a buffer against the Germans.

To block the Helvetian migration, Caesar rushed his legions to Geneva at the grueling pace of ninety miles a day. At Geneva, the Romans destroyed the bridge across the Rhone River and constructed nineteen miles of fortifications. When the Helvetii tried to migrate by another route, Caesar chased them northward and slaughtered them by the thousands.

Caesar and his troops were elated with their success. In battle, the Celts had seemed terrifying at first. They were taller than the Roman legionaries, with painted faces and wild hair. But compared with the Romans, the Celts were disorganized and undisciplined.

The Roman soldiers loved Caesar, this commander who seemed to accomplish miracles through them. Under his urging, they could travel with lightning speed; with him laboring alongside them, they could raise ramparts as if by magic. And Caesar loved his army, which responded to him as beautifully as his favorite warhorse. It was glorious to see thousands of men moving like one organism—at his command.

Caesar next went on the offensive against Ariovistus, leader of a Germanic tribe. Ariovistus was supposedly an ally of Rome, but he had trespassed on the territory of the Sequani, a Celtic tribe under Roman protection. Besides, Caesar's enemies in the Senate were encouraging

Ariovistus to kill him and plotting to turn Caesar's officers against him. They would rather lose Roman territory in Gaul than allow Caesar a chance for military glory.

Knowing all this from his informers in Rome, Caesar deliberately found an excuse to attack the Germans. The battle was fierce, but in the end, Ariovistus was soundly defeated. Caesar's young officer Publius Crassus, a son of Caesar's fellow triumvir Crassus, played an important role in the victory.

Now winter was coming on, so Caesar took his army south to rest and wait for spring. Caesar himself never really took any time off, though. He used the winter months in Cisalpine Gaul to recruit two new legions. This was illegal, since the Roman Senate had not authorized the extra legions. But Caesar was planning a new campaign in northeastern Gaul, where the Belgic tribes were organizing against him. He was confident that if he could conquer new territory for Rome, the Senate would forgive him for breaking the rules.

In the spring, Caesar moved northeast with his much larger army. At first his victories were easy, because the Celts were disorganized and squabbling among themselves. But farther northeast, Caesar's army was ambushed in a forest by a Belgic tribe, the Nervii. The Romans took heavy losses, and it seemed that they would be defeated. Then Caesar, in his scarlet cape and gilded helmet, grabbed a shield from a soldier and plunged into the fight. His men caught their commander's spirit and followed him to win the battle. In the end, the Romans killed almost sixty thousand of the Nervii.

While Caesar was dashing around Gaul with his army, he kept in close touch with Rome. Military couriers raced back and forth, covering the distance between Rome and Caesar's camp in less than a month. He wrote several letters each day, often dictating from horseback, with a secretary riding on each side. He also wrote periodic reports to the Senate on the progress of his campaigns in Gaul.

These reports were meant to impress the Senate with Caesar's valuable service to Rome, but also to let all Roman citizens know that he was protecting the Republic and increasing its wealth. Written in Caesar's clear, forceful style, they made exciting reading for the Romans back home. It was Caesar's Spanish friend Balbus, now a Roman citizen, who published Caesar's accounts of the Gallic Wars in Rome. He also sent Caesar frequent reports from Rome, in code, on the political situation.

Balbus, as well as Caesar's friends and relatives, wrote him about the grand opening of Pompey's Theater, the first permanent theater in Rome. Built of stone on the Field of Mars, it included a temple to Venus Victorious, a public courtyard, and a spacious meeting hall.

Caesar fully expected that while he was off in Gaul for five years, his political enemies would try to destroy him. One of the most dangerous was Cato, the humorless conservative leader who hated everything about Caesar.

Caesar arranged to have the Senate send Cato to the island of Cyprus on a two-year assignment.

Another chief opponent was Marcus Cicero. Convinced that Caesar was a danger to the Republic, Cicero made public speeches attacking the triumvirate. To counteract Cicero's influence, Caesar helped a sworn enemy of Cicero's, Publius Clodius, get elected as the tribune of the people. Through Clodius, Caesar had Cicero charged with treason and forced into exile.

After more than a year of exile, Cicero was allowed to return home. But he found his beautiful mansion on Palatine Hill, as well as his country villas, torn down by Clodius's street gang. Even Caesar felt that Clodius and his gang were getting out of control, and the conservatives encouraged a man named Titus Annius Milo to fight Clodius with a rival gang. As a result, Rome was in the grip of gang warfare.

After Caesar had been in the field for over

two years, he felt that it was time to renew his arrangement with Pompey and Crassus. The two men had never gotten along well, and now their dislike was threatening to dissolve the triumvirate. Caesar couldn't come to Rome to confer with them, because it was against the law for the commander of an army to enter Rome, or even to leave his province. So Caesar called Pompey and Crassus to a meeting in Cisalpine Gaul.

Each of these powerful men still had much to gain from working together. Caesar wanted to keep his governorship of Gaul, and the command of his legions, for another five years. That would give him time to finish the conquest of Gaul and possibly take Britain as well. Then he would be in a prime position to run for consul again.

Meanwhile, Crassus and Pompey would be elected as coconsuls for the next year. Caesar could guarantee their election, because he'd send soldiers to Rome to vote for them. After their year as consuls, Pompey would be granted a five-year governorship of Spain, while Crassus would take over Syria. This governorship would allow Crassus to stage a major military expedition against the Parthians and win the military glory he craved.

The following year, Caesar achieved two brilliant firsts. From eastern Gaul, there was news that German tribes were crossing the Rhine River. Rushing to the border, Caesar had his engineers and soldiers construct a wooden bridge across the Rhine. The Rhine was a wide, deep, swift-running river, and the bridge had to be fifteen hundred feet long and forty feet wide.

But between his gifted military engineers and his highly motivated legionaries, Caesar got the bridge built in record time. From the moment they began to fell the trees to the moment the Roman troops' hobnailed boots tramped across the trestle bridge, only ten days passed. This feat of military engineering proved what talented, capable men Caesar had gathered around him, and how hard they were willing to work for him.

Since there seemed to be no real danger on the Rhine, Caesar turned his army around and marched some two hundred miles to the west, to the English Channel. He had in mind another feat never before accomplished: the conquest of Britain. Very little was known about Britain, and some thought the island didn't even exist. But Caesar was sure that it did, and that it held great wealth in tin and other valuable metals, as well as pearls.

With Caesar during the invasion of Britain was Marcus Cicero's younger brother, Quintus Cicero. Caesar had chosen Quintus as an officer partly because Quintus was a capable and brave man, but partly because this gave Caesar a hold over Marcus Cicero. Cicero had tried to drive a wedge between Pompey and Caesar, but now Cicero was forced to go along with the triumvirate.

On the northern coast of Gaul, Caesar's men were set back at first by their inexperience with the ocean. Romans had sailed the Atlantic only once before, in Caesar's campaign against the bandits in Further Spain. Their ships were not built for the ocean's extreme tides and heavy seas. However, Caesar's fleet managed to land on the southeastern shore of Britain and win a few battles. But at the end of the season, Caesar had to withdraw.

Back in his winter quarters in Cisalpine Gaul, Caesar planned another campaign against Britain for the next summer. He also used the time to plan monuments he wanted to build to himself in Rome. Caesar had in mind something even more impressive than Pompey's Theater: a whole public square next to the present Forum. He would call it the Forum Julia, after his clan name.

The winter also gave Caesar the chance to renew his many friendships in Cisalpine Gaul. At one dinner in Milan, the guests were somehow served asparagus soaked with myrrh, a scent, instead of olive oil. The other guests complained, but Caesar calmly ate a whole dish of the stuff. It was the height of rudeness, Caesar chided his friends, to embarrass the host by pointing out a problem with the food.

The next spring, Caesar returned to Britain with an enormous fleet of new ships, enough to carry five legions and two thousand cavalry. But again, the Britons were not so easy to conquer. Outlandishly dressed in trousers and plaids, they raced their war chariots around the battlefield, attacking and then dashing away. By the end of August, Caesar was concerned by news about rebellion in supposedly conquered Gaul, as well as by rumors from Rome that Pompey intended to become dictator. He decided to leave Britain unconquered.

On Caesar's return to Gaul, terrible news was waiting for him. Julia, only twenty years old, had died in childbirth. And her baby, Caesar's grandchild, had survived only a few days longer.

Caesar put on black clothes and for three days he did not eat, drink, or shave. This loss was even more painful for him than Cornelia's death. Gaius Julius Caesar could command hundreds of thousands of soldiers; he had a network of loyal, highly efficient employees; any number of men and women owed him favors and were eager to return them. But there had been only one Julia to call him "Papa" and love him for himself.

As if this blow were not enough, Aurelia, Caesar's mother, also died shortly afterward. Now there was little left of his most intimate private life.

But even while he grieved, Caesar thought about what Julia's death would mean politically. Julia, loving both her father and her husband and adored by both of them, had been a strong link between Caesar and Pompey. But even before her death, Caesar's informants in Rome had told him that Pompey was drifting toward the conservative faction. Would this be the end of the carefully constructed triumvirate?

Early the next year, Crassus left for his governorship in Syria. He was eager to reach the eastern edge of the empire and launch an attack against the Parthians. He had unrealistic plans to defeat the Parthian Empire and extend the Roman Empire as far as India. But instead, Crassus's army was badly beaten by the Parthians. Both Crassus and his son were killed.

By this time, Caesar was in his winter headquarters in Cisalpine Gaul again. Along with the bad news about Crassus, he heard reports of celebrations in the Gauls' camps. They hated Rome so much that they rejoiced at the defeat of any Roman army, even one that was two thousand miles away.

Even more encouraging to the Gauls, politics in Rome were in dangerous turmoil. Because of the warfare between Clodius and Milo's gangs, elections for consul had not been held during the year 53. Early in 52, Clodius was murdered by Milo. Elections were finally held and resulted in only one consul, Pompey. Many, including Cicero, thought Pompey should be appointed dictator.

Although the triumvirate was over, Caesar tried to create new bonds with Pompey. He proposed that Pompey marry his grandniece, Octavia, and that Caesar should marry Pompey's daughter. But Pompey decided instead to marry the daughter of Metellus Scipio, from an aristocratic and conservative family.

The Gauls, united for once under the chieftain Vercingetorix, chose this time to revolt, attacking the legions that Caesar had left in Gaul. Although it was still winter, Caesar reacted by dashing north with a cavalry force. A mountain pass in his way was blocked with six feet of snow, but Caesar's men had it cleared in twenty-four hours.

The Gallic chieftain Vercingetorix was a charismatic leader and a gifted general, and the struggle between him and Caesar raged over several months. Tribe after tribe of supposedly conquered Gauls went over to Vercingetorix' side. It seemed at first that all Caesar's achievements of the last few years had been for nothing.

However, Caesar pursued Vercingetorix steadily until he cornered him in the fortress of Alesia. Here, Vercingetorix made his last stand with an army of eighty-thousand Gauls. The Romans again produced an amazing engineering feat: a wall twelve feet high and nine miles long, to trap the Gauls. And when another great army of Gauls approached to rescue Vercingetorix, Caesar had his men build a second wall, thirteen miles long, to protect the Romans from the outside.

The fighting at Alesia was bitter and the Romans were greatly outnumbered, but in the end Vercingetorix admitted defeat. Riding out of the gates of Alesia, he laid down his weapons before Caesar in surrender. The outcome of the Gallic Wars was now certain. Caesar had added a vast new territory to the Roman Empire, and he had proved himself as a military genius.

CHAPTER 14

CIVIL WAR

51–46 B.C.

While Gaius Caesar completed the conquest of
Gaul, the Senate back in Rome was paralyzed
with worry. Two powerful, popular, wealthy
commanders of large armies, Caesar and Pompey, seemed to threaten the Republic. Either
one of them might declare himself dictator,
and then king, and end the traditional Roman
system of government. Or Pompey and Caesar
might launch all their military force against
each other, tearing the Republic apart in the
process.

For the moment, Caesar was only asking to
keep his governorship of Gaul, and to be
allowed to run for consul without coming back
to Rome to register as a candidate. He needed

protection from prosecution. Otherwise, his many enemies, led by Cato, would have him arrested the moment he entered the city.

The Senate wanted both Pompey and Caesar to give up command of their armies, but neither general trusted the other. Finally the Senate panicked, decided that Caesar was the more dangerous threat, and passed an emergency decree. They gave Pompey the power to defend Rome. They also voted that Caesar must immediately give up the province of Gaul and his army or else be declared a public enemy. Mark Antony and his fellow tribune, who had worked hard in Rome for Caesar, had to flee the city.

By this time, Caesar had arrived at his winter headquarters in Ravenna with one legion, the Thirteenth. When he heard of the Senate's final decision, he sent his troops south to the border of Cisalpine Gaul, marked by a stream called the Rubicon. He himself went to the baths that day, just as usual, and then sat down to dinner with friends. After dark, he slipped away and took a secret route to meet his troops on the bank of the Rubicon.

Gaius Julius Caesar was used to making quick, forceful decisions. He usually turned out to be right, and he knew that acting quickly could mean the difference between defeat and victory. But here on the bank of the Rubicon, he hesitated. If he entered Italy with his troops, he moved toward war with Pompey. Civil war would mean bloodshed and devastation for thousands of Romans, like the wars between Sulla and Marius that had blighted his youth. Was he willing to inflict this terrible chaos on the Roman people?

But if Caesar accepted the Senate's decree, he would have to flee into exile, or else be tried in Rome and executed as an enemy of the state. After all he had done for Rome! After nine years of brilliant service, after adding the great territory of Gaul, with all its wealth, to the Empire! It was unjust; it was shameful. For his own honor and the honor of his legions, Caesar could not allow it.

With a shrug, Caesar stepped up to the riverbank. "Let the die be cast," he said, shaking a cupped hand as if he were gambling. He *was* gambling—with his own fate, and the fate of Rome. He marched his troops across the Rubicon.

Once in Italy, Caesar moved quickly and easily down the peninsula. Town after town flung open its gates to him, and many more soldiers joined his army. Caesar had solid backing among the middle-class businessmen who ran Italian towns. In the countryside, citizens still remembered Sulla's reign of terror, and they were glad to support Marius's nephew. And it was well known among soldiers that Caesar appreciated and rewarded able men of all classes.

In a few weeks, Caesar had command of eastern Italy almost as far south as Rome. His friends and enemies alike were amazed at his generosity toward the Romans who fought against him. He didn't kill them; he didn't sell them into slavery; he simply let them go. "Let us see," Caesar wrote Balbus, "if by moderation we can win all hearts and secure a lasting victory." He did not want to be a second Sulla, or even a second Marius, taking bloody revenge on his Roman enemies.

Meanwhile, Pompey decided to withdraw from Rome and lead the government to Greece, where he could gather a much larger army. The conservative senators, including Cato, as well as other prominent Romans who thought Pompey would win the civil war, went with him. Caesar chased them all the way to the port of Brundisium, but Pompey's fleet escaped the harbor under cover of night.

It was March, and Caesar was now in control of Italy. Returning to Rome, he reassured the common people by promising them free grain and money. To pay for a grain dole and for the continuing civil war, he raided the state treasury in the Temple of Saturn. He also sent his deputies to Sicily and Sardinia to make sure of grain supplies.

Caesar then set out for Spain, and from June through August he fought with an army commanded by one of Pompey's deputies. When the Pompeian army was finally forced to surrender, Caesar was again generous to his fellow Romans, and let them go.

Back in Rome that autumn, Caesar had to make sure that the government continued to function. The empire must not collapse during his war with Pompey. He had himself appointed dictator for two weeks, until the consular elections could be held.

Elected consul, Caesar was now the legitimate leader of Rome, and Pompey was the outlaw. It was January, a bad time of year for sea travel, and Pompey's well-equipped war galleys patrolled the Adriatic. Pompey was amazed when Caesar nevertheless crossed to Greece, slipping by both the storms and Pompey's fleet.

In March, Caesar's deputy Mark Antony joined him with reinforcements. Caesar's army caught up with Pompey at Dyrrachium, a major port on the Adriatic Sea. In July, Caesar laid siege to the city, and here Pompey inflicted Caesar's worst defeat ever. Caesar himself was almost killed.

After such heavy losses, Caesar was forced to withdraw, but he did not give up. "He who runs may fight again," Caesar quoted from his favorite playwright, Menander. He marched his army across Greece to Thessaly, where he could get reinforcements and supplies.

Following Caesar to Thessaly, Pompey met him in August on the plain of Pharsalus. By this time, it was summer, and the heat was fierce. Pompey's troops outnumbered Caesar's more than two to one, Pompey held the higher ground, and he felt confident of victory.

But on this inland battlefield, Pompey didn't have the support of his warships. Many of his troops were not Romans, but recruits from the eastern provinces. Furthermore, Caesar guessed what Pompey's battle plan would be, and he made his own plan to foil it. This time, it was Pompey's troops who were slaughtered. The rest of his army surrendered, and Pompey fled.

Caesar still did not want to shed Roman blood any more than necessary. He pardoned many of Pompey's officers, and some of them joined his forces. Gaius Cassius Longinus was one, and so was Marcus Brutus, son of Caesar's mistress Servilia.

Caesar sent Mark Antony back to Rome to govern as his deputy. He himself, with a small force, followed Pompey across the Mediterranean Sea to Egypt. In October, Caesar reached Alexandria, the great city founded by Alexander the Great. Caesar's ship was met in the harbor by an Egyptian delegation from Ptolemy XIII. The Egyptians offered gifts: Pompey's signet ring—and his head.

Even after all the treachery and bloodshed Caesar had seen, even after he had thrown all his energy and talent into defeating Pompey Magnus, Caesar was shocked. The Egyptians had assassinated his noble Roman rival because they thought that would please him. Tears came to his eyes.

Pompey was defeated and dead, but Caesar had another reason for staying in the wealthy land of Egypt: to raise money. Also, he saw an opportunity in the power struggle going on within the Ptolemy dynasty. Ptolemy XIII and his older sister, Cleopatra, were supposed to be corulers of Egypt, but instead they were at war.

As for Cleopatra, *she* saw an opportunity in this visit from the ruler of the Roman Empire. She decided to go to Caesar personally and persuade him to support her rather than her brother. But Ptolemy's faction controlled Alexandria. If she went to the palace openly, she would be seized and killed by Ptolemy's men. Cleverly, she had herself rolled into a carpet and delivered to Caesar as a gift.

Caesar was amused and impressed with Cleopatra's daring, and the two hit it off immediately. The Egyptian princess was only twenty-one, but she was just as brilliant, ambitious, and charming as Caesar, the fifty-two-year-old Roman commander. They had much to offer each other. Caesar, as usual, needed money—a great deal of money. Ptolemy XIII refused to give him any of Egypt's vast wealth, but Cleopatra was willing to share. In return, the Roman general could help her defeat her brother and become Queen of Egypt. He could also make sure that Rome treated Egypt as a respected ally instead of a province to be plundered.

Caesar had only a small force with him in Alexandria, but he managed to hold the royal palace against Ptolemy's army for months. He was out of touch with Rome all this time, but it would have been difficult to leave Egypt. At this time of year the winds were blowing across the Mediterranean from the north, the wrong direction for sailing to Italy. Besides, he didn't want to leave without the money he'd come for. Roman reinforcements finally arrived, and Caesar was able to defeat Ptolemy's army. Ptolemy XIII himself was killed.

After a tour of the Nile with Cleopatra, Caesar left Egypt in April. He did not return directly to Rome, but traveled east to Syria to raise still more money. Also, Pharnaces of Pontus, son of Mithridates, was on the march in Asia Minor. After defeating Pharnaces in a single battle, Caesar sent a brief report to Rome: *"Veni, vidi, vici"*—"I came, I saw, I conquered."

In September, Caesar finally returned to Italy. Before he reached Rome, he met with Cicero. Cicero had sided with Pompey in the civil war, and Caesar knew he couldn't really trust him. But he still enjoyed Cicero's witty conversation, and he still wanted to get Cicero to work with him.

In Rome, Caesar found the city in chaos. Poor people were rioting in the streets to protest high rents; gangs roamed at will; and Caesar's deputy Mark Antony had been enjoying high living more than he'd been attending to the affairs of state. The Senate, having lost all the conservative senators when Pompey left, was even feebler than before. Worst of all, Caesar's veteran legions from Gaul were on the point of mutiny. Marching on Rome, they camped on the Field of Mars and demanded rewards.

But in short order Caesar had the government running smoothly again. He decreed that small debts were canceled, and he appointed new senators to fill up the Senate. He also had himself elected consul, along with his deputy Marcus Aemilius Lepidus, for the next year, so that there would be no doubt about who was in charge.

As for the mutinous soldiers, Caesar spoke to the assembled troops on the Field of Mars. Assuring them that they would receive their rewards, he declared that they were now discharged from his army. He addressed them as "citizens," implying that they had given up their right to be called "legionaries." And of course they wouldn't march through Rome in Caesar's victory parade.

The soldiers suddenly remembered how

proud they were of their military service, and how Caesar had always shared their hardships and treated them with respect. They had followed him back and forth across the Alps, bridged wide rivers, built fortifications overnight. With Caesar as their commander, they had risked death and won fierce battles. Now they cried out, begging his forgiveness and pleading to be allowed to remain his legionaries.

All that settled, Caesar left for Africa again in December. Even though Pompey himself was dead, Pompey's sons and Caesar's longtime enemy Cato had gathered a large army. In spite of his smaller army and a shortage of supplies, Caesar defeated the Pompeians. Cato committed suicide. But it was a grim victory for Caesar, because thousands of the corpses on the battlefield were his fellow Romans. Some of them were even men he'd already pardoned once, who had promised not to oppose him again.

Returning to Rome at the end of July,

Caesar was now determined to celebrate a triumph. His most recent victories were actually in the civil war with Pompey and his followers, but Caesar had no intention of triumphing over his fellow Romans. Instead, he would celebrate his conquests of Gaul, Egypt, Pontus, and Africa.

The celebrations in Rome, lasting for forty days, included public banquets, plays, gladiatorial games, a grand opening of the Forum Julia, and four magnificent parades. The first parade celebrated the conquest of Gaul. The Gallic leader Vercingetorix, who had been in prison ever since his surrender at Alesia, was exhibited in that procession. The streets of Rome along the parade route were decked with flowers, and music and perfume filled the air.

The crowds shouted out praise to Caesar in his chariot, wearing the victor's laurel wreath. Caesar's grandnephew, Octavius, marched behind the chariot, customarily the place for a general's son. Caesar's legions followed, bursting with pride. This one day of all days, it was their right to roast their commander by singing insulting songs, and they roared out the verses. Listening to his men, Caesar had to repress a smile. The *least* insulting thing they said about him was that he was bald.

CHAPTER 15

THE DICTATOR

46–44 B.C.

Now that Caesar was firmly in charge of Rome, he made some improvements that he'd had in mind for a long time. He ordered the construction of public libraries, the first in Rome. He reformed the calendar, with the consultation of the astronomer Sosigenes of Alexandria. Instead of basing the year on lunar months, which required frequent addition and subtraction to keep in sync, he decreed that calendar would be based on the solar year of 365 ¼ days.

Such reforms were satisfying, but Caesar had little time to enjoy them. Pompey's sons, having escaped after their defeat in Africa, led an uprising in Spain. Only a few weeks after the celebrations in Rome, Caesar left for Spain.

He took with him his grandnephew Octavius, now eighteen. Caesar was very fond of Julia Minor's grandson, a good-looking and well-spoken lad, with a natural instinct for politics.

As in Africa, it was bitter fighting, Romans against Romans. The years of bloodshed were finally overwhelming Caesar—he felt downhearted, instead of elated and energized, before the crucial battle. But again he was victorious, at the cost of slaying thirty thousand Romans. He stayed on in Spain to settle and reorganize the province. It was September, a year after his triumph, before he returned to Rome.

By this time, Caesar was not in good health. Even before he left for Spain, he'd been suffering from headaches and fainting spells. Now he wrote his will. He made his grandnephew Octavius the heir to his estate. Octavius was studying in Greece, where he'd gone after the Spanish campaign.

In spite of all the enemies Caesar had killed, he still had enemies among his own class, the senators of Rome. He tried to create good feeling by various means, including having Pompey's statues put up around Rome again. Although Caesar and Pompey had fought to the death, Caesar would be generous and honor Pompey Magnus as a hero.

Cicero did not dare openly oppose Caesar, but he was convinced that Caesar had destroyed the republican government of Rome. Instead of reforming the Roman constitution, Caesar was ruling as a dictator. In February, he assumed the title Dictator for Life. There were rumors that he wanted to be crowned king.

Not only that, but Caesar seemed to want to be worshipped as a god. There were already temples dedicated to him in Greece; and in Rome, statues of Caesar were placed in temples to other gods. The seventh month, Quintilis, was renamed after his clan name, Julius, as though he were equal to the deities Mars (March) or Juno (June). Caesar's image appeared on Roman coins, which had never before been done while a ruler was alive. Senators were outraged that

Caesar wore his victory robes to conduct meetings of the Senate, and that he sat down before them like a king. Caesar explained that he had to sit because of his fits of dizziness, but many did not believe him.

There was a whole cluster of nasty rumors around Caesar and Cleopatra. The Egyptian queen had come to live outside Rome, on the western bank of the Tiber River, in a palace Caesar had built for her. Did he intend to marry her? Romans were appalled at the mere fact that a woman ruled Egypt, let alone that this woman might have some influence on the rule of Rome. Another rumor was that Caesar would soon acknowledge Cleopatra's son, Caesarion, as his heir, and move the capital of the empire from Rome to Alexandria.

Romans were also uneasy that Caesar was planning to leave soon on an ambitious eastern campaign. He wanted to subdue the Parthians, to revenge their defeat of Crassus. But did Rome really need the expense and bloodshed of a new war?

During the year before, a conspiracy, led by Gaius Cassius Longinus, had begun to develop. The conspirators had different motives: Some of them wanted revenge for their relatives, killed in the civil war. Some of them resented Caesar because he hadn't given them the rewards they wanted. Some of them, like the idealistic Marcus Brutus, believed that the glorious Roman Republic could be restored if only Caesar was removed. But all of them wanted Gaius Julius Caesar dead.

Strangely, Caesar seemed to be making it easier for the conspirators. He knew of plots against his life, but he didn't have anyone arrested. He had a bodyguard of fiercely loyal Spaniards, but he dismissed them. One day when Caesar was presiding over a sacrifice, a soothsayer named Spurinna told him to beware of danger on or before the Ides of March, the fifteenth day of the month. Caesar only smiled. He didn't need a soothsayer to tell him that danger lurked around every corner.

On the night of March 14, the conspirators

made their final plans. In another part of the city, Caesar arrived at his deputy Lepidus's house for dinner. He ate and drank only a little. He had never indulged much in food, and even less so these days, when his health was poor.

It seemed now that he'd won the struggle to rule the Roman Empire, Caesar had lost his zest for life. It was clear that he would never succeed in reforming the Republic. The conservative senators were too devoted to tradition, and too attached to their own privileges, to give up any power to other classes. Since Caesar couldn't win over the Senate to work with him, he would keep control of the state and make improvements by decree.

Worst of all, Caesar was lonely. The people he had loved most deeply were gone: Aurelia, Cornelia, Julia. He looked forward to the Parthian campaign. Octavius, his blood relative and heir, would join him in Macedonia. Caesar would be surrounded by legions who would gladly die for him, and the enemies he killed would not be Romans.

At Lepidus's dinner, the conversation turned to the question What is the best way to die? Caesar looked up from the letters he was signing—as usual, he was doing more than one thing at a time. "The best way to die," he said, "is quickly and unexpectedly."

The next morning Caesar was supposed to preside over a meeting of the Senate in the hall connected to Pompey's Theater. It was to be the Dictator's last meeting with the Senate before he left on March 18 for Parthia. He was feeling worse than usual, and he almost cancelled the meeting. But one of the conspirators, Decimus Brutus, came to his residence and persuaded him to attend.

As Caesar stepped out of his litter in front of Pompey's Theater, a Greek acquaintance handed him a note. Caesar tucked the note in his toga to read later. It warned him against an attack planned for today.

At the door of the Senate hall, Caesar caught sight of the soothsayer Spurinna and remembered his prophecy. He had an impulse to tease the man. "The Ides of March have come," he pointed out.

"Yes, Caesar," said Spurinna without smiling, "but they are not yet gone."

Caesar's deputy Mark Antony was with him outside the hall, but one of the conspirators kept him talking on some pretext. Caesar entered by himself and sat down in his gilded chair.

The conspirators came up to Caesar with knives hidden in their togas, pretending to petition him. One of them seized his toga and pulled it away from his throat and chest. That was the agreed-upon signal for the rest to attack.

At first Caesar fought fiercely, although his only weapon was his metal stylus. Then, weakened by stab after stab, he realized that this was the end. Caesar pulled his toga over his head so that at least he would die in a dignified way. He fell at the foot of Pompey's statue.

The conspirators had intended to bring back the Roman Republic, but instead they plunged the country into another civil war. The common people of Rome, with whom Caesar had been very popular, rioted for weeks. Mark Antony hunted down and killed many of the conspirators. He also had Cicero killed, although Cicero had not actually taken part in the conspiracy.

Caesar's loyal staff rallied behind Octavius, in spite of his youth, and he changed his name to Gaius Julius Caesar Octavianus, to underline the fact that he was Caesar's heir. Octavian, Mark Antony, and Lepidus joined forces. In 42 B.C., their armies defeated Brutus and Cassius's troops at the Battle of Philippi. Octavius, Antonius, and Lepidus as the Second Triumvirate then divided the empire, and Antony ruled his territory from Egypt with Cleopatra. But finally Octavian defeated Antony and Cleopatra and emerged as the sole ruler of the Roman Empire.

In 30 B.C., Octavian became the first Roman emperor, calling himself Caesar Augustus. He not only made himself ruler for life, but also established a dynasty to rule after him. He had himself and Julius Caesar declared gods, to be worshipped throughout the empire.

It has been many centuries since anyone sacrificed to the divine Julius, but the influence of Gaius Julius Caesar's life still shapes today's world. His conquest of Gaul spread Greco-Roman culture and the Latin language over the continent of Western Europe. Although Caesar hadn't added Britain to the empire, through his invasion he had pushed out the edge of the known world. The Roman Empire, organized by Caesar Augustus into a highly efficient system of government, ruled the known world for almost five hundred years. The Empire in turn allowed the rapid spread of Christianity, which the emperor Constantine made the religion of the Empire in A.D. 313.

Gaius Julius Caesar's family name, Caesar, became a word meaning "supreme ruler." Two thousand years later, it would still be used that way by the Germans ("kaiser") and the Russians ("tsar"). Napoleon Bonaparte studied Caesar's war diaries, and he thought of himself as a new Caesar. Caesar is still considered one of the great military geniuses of all time, and his record of the Gallic Wars is read by generals as well as historians.

We still use the solar calendar that Caesar established, which was slightly adjusted in the sixteenth century by Pope Gregory XIII. And we still honor the month of Gaius Julius Caesar's birth, calling it "July."

FOR MORE INFORMATION

VIDEOS

Cromwell Productions, 1999. *The Legions of Rome: The Gallic Wars.*
Includes vivid dramatizations of Celtic warriors in battle, as well as explanations of campaigns and key battles.

Turner Home Entertainment; PBS Home Video, 1995. *Roman City.*
Based on the book *City,* by David Macaulay. Clear, engaging demonstrations of aspects of Roman urban life.

BOOKS

Grant, Michael. *Julius Caesar.* New York: M. Evans & Company, Inc., 1992.

Brief but thorough biography by a leading
historian.

Payne, Robert. *The Horizon Book of Ancient
Rome*. New York: American Heritage
Publishing Company, 1966.
Heavily illustrated, readable overview of
Roman history and culture. Many maps,
battle plans, and literary selections.

ON THE INTERNET

http://heraklia.fws1.com
Julius Caesar: The Last Dictator
An introduction to Gaius Julius Caesar
and his times.

http://www.vroma.org
VRoma
A virtual community for teaching and
learning Latin and ancient Roman culture.

http://penelope.uchicago.edu/Thayer/E/
Roman/home.html
LacusCurtius: Into the Roman World
A major site on Roman antiquity.

FOR ADULT READERS

Everitt, Anthony. *Cicero: The Life and Times of Rome's Greatest Politician.* New York: Random House, 2001.
Very well written, and illuminating about Caesar as well as Cicero.

Kahn, Arthur D. *The Education of Julius Caesar: A Biography, a Reconstruction.* New York: Schocken Books, 1986.
A lively, detailed, provocative biography.

Saylor, Steven. The Roma Sub Rosa series (*Roman Blood,* etc.). New York: St. Martin's Press, 1991–2005.
Mysteries set in ancient Rome during the period of Julius Caesar's lifetime. Engaging and entertaining, but also extremely accurate historical fiction.

★★★ # Childhood of Famous Americans ★★★

One of the most popular series ever published for young Americans, these classics have been praised alike by parents, teachers, and librarians. With these lively, inspiring, fictionalized biographies—easily read by children of eight and up—today's youngster is swept right into history.

ABIGAIL ADAMS ★ JOHN ADAMS ★ LOUISA MAY ALCOTT ★ SUSAN B. ANTHONY ★ NEIL ARMSTRONG ★ CRISPUS ATTUCKS ★ CLARA BARTON ★ ELIZABETH BLACKWELL ★ DANIEL BOONE ★ BUFFALO BILL ★ ROBERTO CLEMENTE ★ DAVY CROCKETT ★ JOE DIMAGGIO ★ WALT DISNEY ★ AMELIA EARHART ★ THOMAS A. EDISON ★ ALBERT EINSTEIN ★ HENRY FORD ★ BENJAMIN FRANKLIN ★ LOU GEHRIG ★ GERONIMO ★ ALTHEA GIBSON ★ JOHN GLENN ★ JIM HENSON ★ HARRY HOUDINI ★ LANGSTON HUGHES ★ ANDREW JACKSON ★ MAHALIA JACKSON ★ THOMAS JEFFERSON ★ HELEN KELLER ★ JOHN FITZGERALD KENNEDY ★ MARTIN LUTHER KING JR. ★ ROBERT E. LEE ★ MERIWETHER LEWIS ★ ABRAHAM LINCOLN ★ MARY TODD LINCOLN ★ THURGOOD MARSHALL ★ JOHN MUIR ★ ANNIE OAKLEY ★ JACQUELINE KENNEDY ONASSIS ★ ROSA PARKS ★ MOLLY PITCHER ★ POCAHONTAS ★ RONALD REAGAN ★ PAUL REVERE ★ JACKIE ROBINSON ★ KNUTE ROCKNE ★ MR. ROGERS ★ ELEANOR ROOSEVELT ★ FRANKLIN DELANO ROOSEVELT ★ TEDDY ROOSEVELT ★ BETSY ROSS ★ WILMA RUDOLPH ★ BABE RUTH ★ SACAGAWEA ★ SITTING BULL ★ JIM THORPE ★ HARRY S. TRUMAN ★ SOJOURNER TRUTH ★ HARRIET TUBMAN ★ MARK TWAIN ★ GEORGE WASHINGTON ★ MARTHA WASHINGTON ★ LAURA INGALLS WILDER ★ WILBUR AND ORVILLE WRIGHT

★★★ # Collect them all! ★★★